T0135663

New Algorithms for Learning of Mixture Models and Their Application for Classification and Density Estimation

Bambang Heru Iswanto, M.Sc.

Gedruckt mit Unterstützung des Deutschen Akademischen Austausdienstes

Bibliografische Information Der Deutschen Bibliothek

Die Deutsche Bibliothek verzeichnet diese Publikation in der Deutschen Nationalbibliografie; detaillierte bibliografische Daten sind im Internet über http://dnb.ddb.de abrufbar.

ISBN 3-8325-0809-0

Logos Verlag Berlin
Comeniushof, Gubener Str. 47,
10243 Berlin
Tel.: +49 030 42 85 10 90
Fax: +49 030 42 85 10 92
INTERNET: http://www.logos-verlag.de

New Algorithms for Learning of Mixture Models and Their Application for Classification and Density Estimation

vorgelegt von

Bambang Heru Iswanto, M.Sc.

Fakultät IV Elektrotechnik und Informatik
der Technischen Universität Berlin
zur Erlangung des akademischen Grades

Doktor der Naturwissenschaften
– Dr. rer. nat –

genehmigte Dissertation

Promotionsausschuss:
Vorsitzender : Prof. Dr. Ulrich Kockelkorn
Berichter   : Prof. Dr. Klaus Obermayer
Berichter   : Prof. Dr. Fritz Wysotzki

Tag der wissenschaftlichen Aussprache: 10. Dezember 2004

Berlin 2005

D 83

Für meinen Bruder und meine Familie

Contents

1 Introduction   1

   1.1 Semi-Supervised Learning   4

   1.2 Active Learning   6

2 Mixture Models and EM Algorithm   9

   2.1 Mixture Models   9

   2.2 Maximum-Likelihood   12

   2.3 EM Algorithm   13

      2.3.1 E-Step   14

      2.3.2 M-Step   16

3 Mixture Models for Classification   19

   3.1 Classification   20

   3.2 Classification Learning   21

   3.3 Optimal Decision Rule   24

   3.4 Model-Based Classifiers   25

   3.5 Supervised Learning of Mixture Models   26

3.5.1   Learning of Simple Models   26

3.5.2   Learning of Complex Models   28

4   LBGU-EM Algorithm for Density Estimation   **35**

4.1   Initialization of EM   36

4.2   LBG-U Algorithm   38

4.3   LBGU-EM Algorithm   40

4.4   Experimental Results   41

4.5   Conclusion   43

5   Classification Using Labeled and Unlabeled Data   **47**

5.1   Related Work   50

5.2   Semi-Supervised Learning   52

5.2.1   Learning of Simple Models   53

5.2.2   Learning of Complex Models   57

5.3   EM with Regularized Weighting Factor   61

5.4   Experimental Results   64

5.4.1   Experiments Without Weighting Factors   67

5.4.2   Experiments With Weighting Factors   71

5.5   Conclusion   73

6   Active Learning for Mixture Model-based
Classifiers   **79**

6.1   What is Active Learning?   80

6.2   Generative Classifiers: A Review   84

6.3   Active Leaning using Expected Likelihood-based Sampling   86

6.3.1   Description of Algorithm   88

6.3.2   Experimental Results   90

6.3.3   Conclusion   97

6.4   Active Leaning using Likelihood-Increasing Sampling . . .   98

6.4.1   Description of Algorithm   98

6.4.2 Experimental Results 103

6.4.3 Conclusion 107

7 Summary   **111**

References   **117**

List of Algorithms

1   General EM algorithm 15

2   EM algorithm for mixture models 17

3   EM algorithm of the mixture models for multiple components per class 34

4   LBG algorithm (Linde *et al.*, 1980) 39

5   LBG-U algorithm (Fritzke, 1997) 40

6   Semi-supervised learning of GMM 57

7   Semi-supervised learning of complex models 62

8   Semi-supervised learning using regularized weighting factors 65

9   General approach of active learning 81

10   Active learning using Expected Likelihood-based Sampling (ELS) 91

11   Active learning using Likelihood-Increasing Sampling (LIS) 101

List of Figures

3.1 Model learning from examples (Vapnik, 1998). 22

4.1 (a) Two-dimensional data, data set A. (b) Three-dimensional data, data set B. 42

4.2 Mean of negative log-likelihood and variance values for dataset A. 43

4.3 Mean of negative log-likelihood and variance values for dataset B. 44

4.4 Mean of negative log-likelihood and variance values for dataset C. 45

5.1 Plot of training data sets. Data points of the same class are shown using the same color. (a) 2GAUSS data set generated from two gaussian densities, $M = 2[1, 1]$, with the same variance. (b) PARACHUTE data set, each class was generated from five gaussian densities, $M = 10[5, 5]$, with the same variance. 67

5.2 Generalization error of classifiers using PARACHUTE data set and correct models ($M = 10[5, 5]$). Experiments used different number of labeled data points: 50, 80, and 100. **Horizontal axis**: amount of unlabeled data used. **Vertical-axis**: generalization error of classifiers. Error bars represent one standard error of the mean. 68

5.3   Generalization error of classifier trained using 2GAUSS data
      set with different model complexity. **Horizontal axis**:
      amount of unlabeled data used. **Vertical-axis**: generali-
      zation error. Error bars represent one standard error of the
      mean. Experiments were conducted using different number
      of mixture components per class: 2[1, 1] (correct model),
      6[3, 3], and 10[5, 5]. All experiments used 100 labeled data
      points.   69

5.4   Generalization error of classifier trained using PARACHUTE
      data set with different model complexity. **Horizontal
      axis**: amount of unlabeled data used. **Vertical-axis**:
      generalization error. Error bars represent one standard
      error of the mean. Experiments were conducted using dif-
      ferent number of mixture components per class: 2[1, 1],
      4[2, 2], 6[3, 3], 10[5, 5] (correct model), 14[7, 7], 20[10, 10]
      and 90[45, 45]. All experiments used 100 labeled data
      points.   70

5.5   Performance of classifiers with different model complex-
      ity when 2GAUSS data set and the regularized weighting
      factors are used. The weighting factor of unlabeled data
      was varied to the values: λ_u = 0.1, 1.0, 2.0, and 5.0,
      while weighting factor of labeled data is set to one (λ_l =
      1). **Horizontal-axis**: amount of unlabeled data used.
      Vertical-axis: generalization error. Error bars represent
      one standard error of the mean. Some experiments were
      conducted for different model complexity: (a) $M = 2[1, 1]$
      (**correct model**) with 20 labeled examples; (b) $M =$
      6[3, 3] with 60 labeled examples; (c) $M = 10[5, 5]$ with
      100 labeled examples. Here the size of labeled data was
      set 10 labeled data points for one component.   74

5.6   Performance of classifiers with different model complex-
      ity when PARACHUTE data set and the regularized weigh-
      ting factors are used. The weighting factor of unlabeled
      data was varied to the values: $\lambda_u = 0.1$, 1.0, 2.0, and
      5.0, while weighting factor of labeled data is set to one
      ($\lambda_l = 1$). **Horizontal-axis**: amount of unlabeled data
      used. **Vertical-axis**: generalization error. Error bars
      represent one standard error of the mean. Some experi-
      ments were conducted for different model complexity: (a)
      $M = 2[1,1]$, (b) $M = 6[3,3]$, (c) $M = 10[5,5]$ (**correct
      model**), (d) $M = 14[7,7]$. For all experiments were con-
      ducted using 100 labeled data points.   75

6.1   Illustration of query selections using the *Expected-Likelihood-
      based Sampling* (**ELS**) algorithm. (a) The query process is
      begun by employing a weak model initialized using six la-
      beled examples. The arrow points to an informative exam-
      ple selected for querying from the pool according to the
      current model. (b) The selected query after labeling and
      added to training set for next queries. The new example
      expanded covariance of the gaussian (blue, right side). (c)
      The model after two new examples added to the training
      set. The selected examples expanded covariance of both
      gaussians, so that the model covers the data set. The
      graph of (d) and (e) show the distribution of selected exam-
      ples, centers and covariance of the gaussians after 6 and
      34 queries, respectively. An interesting graph is shown in
      (d), in which a perfect decision boundary (black line) was
      achieved using only six queries.   89

6.2   Two dimensional synthetic data sets. **Left**: 2GAUSS data
      set consisting of 400 data points. **Right**: BANANA con-
      sisting of 400 data points, has zero mean and standard
      deviation one.   92

6.3 The result of experiment using the *Expected Likelihood-based Sampling* method using 2GAUSS data sets and a pool of 400 examples. **Horizontal-axis**: the number of queries. **Vertical-axis**: generalization error. Error bars represent one standard error of the mean. In this experiment, the classifiers were built using gaussian mixture models with different number of component densities: $M = 2[1,1]$ and $10[5,5]$.   93

6.4 The result of experiment using the *Expected Likelihood-based Sampling* method using BANANA data sets and a pool of 400 examples. **Horizontal-axis**: the number of queries. **Vertical-axis**: generalization error. Error bars represent one standard error of the mean. In this experiment, the classifiers were built using gaussian mixture models with different number of component densities: $M = 2[1,1]$, $14[7,7]$ and $20[10,10]$.   94

6.5 The result of experiment using the *Expected Likelihood-based Sampling* method and random selection on the HEART data set. The experiment was performed using a pool of unlabeled examples of 170 examples. **Horizontal-axis**: the number of queries. **Vertical-axis**: generalization error. Error bars represent one standard error of the mean. In this experiment, the classifiers were built using generative models with different number of component densities: $M = 2[1,1], 4[2,2]$ and $10[5,5]$.   95

6.6 The result of experiment using the *Expected Likelihood-based Sampling* method and random selection on the DIABETES data set. The experiment was performed using a pool of unlabeled examples of 468 examples. **Horizontal-axis**: the number of queries. **Vertical-axis**: generalization error. Error bars represent one standard error of the mean. In this experiment, the classifiers were built using generative models with different number of component densities: $M = 4[2,2], 6[3,3]$ and $10[5,5]$.   96

6.7   Illustration of query selections using the *Likelihood In-creasing Sampling* (LIS) method. The simulation shows how the LIS method selects new examples when 2GAUSS data set is used for training. Here, we take simplest mo-del that consists of two gaussian densities with spherical covariance parameters. In graph (a) the query process is begun by employing a weak model initialized using six la-beled examples. In (b) a new example with the highest average likelihood is selected to be labeled and added to training set for next queries. The model after two new la-beled examples added to the training set is showed in graph (c). The selected examples moved the center of gaussians to the position near centers of actual distribution. The graph of (d) shows the distribution of selected examples, centers and covariance of the gaussians after 30 queries. .   102

6.8   The result of experiment of the *Likelihood-Increasing Sam-pling* method using 2GAUSS data sets. **Horizontal-axis**: the number of queries. **Vertical-axis**: generalization error. In this experiment, the classifiers were built using $M = 2$ gaussian mixture components and initialized with five la-beled examples for each class. The error bars denote the standard deviation about the mean of 50 trials.   105

6.9   The result of experiment of the *Likelihood-Increasing Sam-pling* method using BANANA data sets. **Horizontal-axis**: the number of queries. **Vertical-axis**: generalization error. In this experiment, the classifiers were built using $M = 10[5, 5]$ gaussian mixture components and initialized with 25 labeled examples for each class. The error bars denote the standard deviation about the mean of 50 trials for both the Likelihood-Increasing Sampling and the passive method. 106

6.10 The result of experiment of the *Likelihood-Increasing Sampling* method using HEART data sets. **Horizontal-axis**: the number of queries. **Vertical-axis**: generalization error. In this experiment, the classifiers were built using mixture of two gaussians and given 10 labeled examples for initialization. The error bars denote the standard deviation about the mean of 30 trial for all, *Likelihood-Increasing Sampling*, random selection and *Expected Likelihood-based Sampling* method. In this experiment, *Likelihood-Increasing Sampling* used only 100 of 170 available unlabeled data in the pool for querying. 108

List of Symbols

$\mathcal{A}$	set of units represent clusters
$\mathcal{E}$	statistical expectation operator
E	quantization error
$\mathcal{D}$	input sequence of training example
$\mathcal{D}_l$	input sequence of labeled example
$\mathcal{D}_u$	input sequence of unlabeled example
$\mathbf{I}$	identity matrix
L	likelihood
$\mathcal{L}$	log-likelihood
λ	regularization parameter
$\boldsymbol{\mu}$	center of gaussian
∇	gradient operator
N	size of training sample
$p(\boldsymbol{x})$	unconditional probability of input $\boldsymbol{x}$
π	mixing parameter of mixture model
$\phi(\boldsymbol{x})$	mixture component
$\phi(\boldsymbol{x}, \alpha)$	classifier parameterized by α
$\boldsymbol{\Psi}$	mixture model parameter
$P(C_k|\boldsymbol{x})$	posterior probability of class C_k give input $\boldsymbol{x}$
$\boldsymbol{\Sigma}$	covariance matrix
$\mathbf{M}^{-1}$	inverse of matrix $\mathbf{M}$
$\mathbf{M}^T$	transpose of matrix $\mathbf{M}$

σ^2	variance
$\tau(C_k|\boldsymbol{x})$	posterior probability of class C_k give input $\boldsymbol{x}$
θ	kernel density parameter
$\mathcal{V}$	Voronoi set
$\mathbf{w}$	reference vector
$\boldsymbol{y}$	class label
$\boldsymbol{z}$	class label
z_{ji}	indicator variable
$\in$	symbol for "belong to"
$\cup$	symbol for "union of"

Minima and Maxima

1. The symbol $\arg\min_c f(c)$ signifies the minimum of the function $f(c)$ with respect to the argument c

2. The symbol $\arg\max_c f(c)$ signifies the maximum of the function $f(c)$ with respect to the argument c

Preface

Mixture model is known as a convenient way for modelling the probability density function in statistics. Recently, the mixture model is adopted by machine learning communities in a variety of application settings including classification, density estimation, cluster analysis, images processing and function approximation. Mixture models are also relevant to be applied to many aspect of neural computing, for example for estimating data distribution in the input space of radial basis function networks.

This dissertation concerns with learning algorithms of the mixture model, especially for density estimation and classification tasks. In many situation, however, the existing learning methods require a large number of labeled training data to learn the classifiers accurately. Unfortunately, in almost all practical situation the procuring of class labels is very expensive.

Furthermore, alternative learning methods are investigated. The methods are of two different approaches, namely semi-supervised learning and active learning. In the first approach, classifiers are trained using training data sets that consist of labeled and unlabeled data. While in the second approach we select carefully which unlabeled data points which should be queried for labeling and adding into training labeled data set.

I tried to make the presentation as self-contained as possible. Due to a lack of space, however, I had to omit details, which might be necessary for a full understanding. After the first chapter that provides an introduction to the motivation and aims of the dissertation, readers can continue to read next chapters. For readers not familiar with the problem of modelling the probability distribution I suggest to start reading in Chapter 2, which gives a brief review of mixture model, maximum-likelihood and EM algorithm.

Chapter 3 deals with constructing generative classifiers using mixture models and incomplete data problems, as well as discussing proposed techniques based on EM algorithm. We present learning algorithms for simple and complex models, in which multiple mixture components are used to represent a class of the data.

Thereafter, in Chapter 4 we consider learning problems of mixture models, especially the initialization problem of EM. We present the LBGU-EM algorithm, a learning algorithm to remedy the problem. An empirical study that compare the performances of EM using random-, LBG- (a.k.a $k-$means) and LBGU-initialization also will be presented.

Chapter 5 focuses on the semi-supervised learning problems using mixture models-based classifiers. In this chapter we consider effect of the additional unlabeled data on generalization of classifiers. Special attention is given to study the effect on model complexity, overfitting condition and regularization. We present also a novel regularization method of labeled/unlabeled data using *regularized* weighting factors.

Chapter 6 constitutes our contributions on active learning techniques for generative classifiers based on gaussian mixture models. We present two novel active learning methods, namely active learning using the Expected Likelihood-based Sampling (ELS) and the Likelihood-Increasing Sampling (LIS). Both methods aim to reduce the size of labeled data set to construct the generative classifiers by choosing carefully training data sets. Finally, conclusions are presented in Chapter 7.

Acknowledgements

First of all I am deeply indebted to my principal advisor, Prof. Dr. Klaus Obermayer (Neural Information Processing group, Technical University of Berlin), who provided not only scientific and moral support, but also gave an opportunity to continue my PhD research in Technical University of Berlin. I was fortunate enough to be a member of this research group, where I have been introduced with statistical learning theory which is fundamental in the field of machine learning.

I would like to thank to my previous advisor, Dr.-Ing. Habil. Berd Fritzke for his two years guidance during my PhD research in the Neuroinformatik group, Dresden University of Technology before he left it. From him I have learned the neural networks and data mining technology, which is very helpful for further research at Technical University of Berlin.

Special thanks to Prof. Dr. Ulrich Kockelkorn for chairing the committee in the defence and his constructive correction of the statistical part of my dissertation. Also, I would like to express my thank to Prof. Dr. Fritz Wisotzky for reviewing the present dissertation.

Most of this work has been done at Neural Information Processing group, Technical University of Berlin. I would like to thank all current and former members of this group. First, I would like to mention Theory Club members Dr. Sepp Hochreiter, Holger Schöner, André Paus, Roland Vollgraf and Sambu Seo with whom I had interesting discussion about machine learning theory. I take particular pleasure in mentioning Dr. Sepp Hochreiter for his advice to solve some problems and corrections in preparation of this dissertation. Also many thanks go to Gregor Wenning for his helpful tips and Susanne Schönknecht for her correction in german language. I particularly thank Hendrik Purwins and Oliver Beck for the opportunity to use their computer any time I need. Thanks due to Nabil Lashin for sharing the room and discussions with topics ranging from religion, politic to daily life in Germany. Also I would like to thanks Johannes Mohr, Kamil Adiloglu, Muamar Ahmad, Steffen Grnewlder, Thomas Hoch, Andr Przywara, Waldemar Rhoden, Claudia Sanelli, Lars Schwabe, Peter Wiesing, Klaus Wimmer and Joshua Young for their cooperative and friendship.

Several other people contributed to this dissertation in one way or another. I particularly thank Noer Azam Achsani for many helpful discussion on statistics and his support to finish this dissertation. Many thanks go to Martin (Bessy, Germany) for his help to translate the summary part to german. I would like to thank my colleagues in Department of Physics, Jakarta State University for their supports.

Appreciation is sincerely expressed to the Indonesian Government through PGSM Project and DAAD for supporting this research financially.

I am particularly grateful to my brother Subandrio HS for his motivation and supports during my study. Special appreciation goes to my wife, Erlinda, for her understanding, patience and willingness to accompany me to Berlin. Without their constant love, support and encouragement I would never been able to produce this dissertation. Much love also to our son, Herbian Alfarisi Iswanto.

Wedding, Berlin   BAMBANG HERU ISWANTO
December 2004

CHAPTER 1
Introduction

One of the important aspects in the human pattern recognition is its capability to learn. In many situations human can easily recognize new particular objects after some similar objects have been learnt before. It is natural that we should seek to design and build machines that can recognize intelligently patterns as human. An emerging field in the artificial intelligence concerning with the study of methods for programming computers to learn is the *machine learning* (Mitchell, 1997; Dietterich, 2003). Learning in this context is understood as inductive inference, where one observes examples that represent incomplete information, which typically be a set of empirical data obtained from repeated measurements. The learning can be seen as building an abstraction of a phenomenon that yields a complete and robust description of its interesting concepts.

There are two major paradigms of learning in the field of machine learning: *supervised learning* and *unsupervised learning*.

In the supervised learning, learning machines are provided "training" examples that consist of pairs of input and output data to learn a mapping from input space to output space so that able to predict output values for new input data as well. The output may be the values of continuous or discrete variables. When the output represents continuous variables the supervised learning is related to *regression* tasks. The supervised learning is related to *classification* tasks when the outputs are discrete and represent class labels or categories. A pair consisting of an input and its associated class is called a *labeled* example. The problem of face and fingerprint recognition (Jain *et al.*, 2004), speech recognition (Sixtus *et al.*, 2000) and text classification (McCallum & Nigam, 1998) are prototypical tasks of supervised classification.

In the other paradigm, termed unsupervised learning (Ripley, 1996; Bishop, 1995), the learning machine is provided with only the input data, without desired outputs for them. As the name implies, this type of learning does not intend to map input into output space, but to observe presupposed structure from a given data set according to the specific criteria. There are a wide range of unsupervised learning tasks, e.g. cluster analysis (Jain & Dubes, 1988), vector quantization (Linde *et al.*, 1980; Kohonen, 2001), data visualization (Simula *et al.*, 1999; Kohonen, 2001), independent component analysis (Jutten & Heraut, 1991; Amari *et al.*, 1995) and density estimation (Devroye *et al.*, 1996; McLachlan & Basford, 1988).

In many situations, however, success of a learning depends on some factors one of them is the data set at the learners disposal. In the classification tasks, the existing supervised learning methods including both *discriminative* (e.g. Support Vector Machines and linear logistic regression) and *generative classifiers* (e.g. mixture models based classifiers and Naive Bayes classifiers) usually require a large number of labeled training data to learn accurately. Performance of classifiers normally improves with larger labeled data sets. Unfortunately, in many practical settings, only small size of the given data are labeled and most of them are unlabeled, i.e. which have not been classified by a human beforehand. Furthermore, labeling of data may be expensive because it must be often done by experts and requires expensive resources, such as laboratory tests and labeling of medical data. In many situations, the labeling is also time consuming, for example the labeling of documents and web pages. In the other side, obtaining large quantities of unlabeled data are very easy and cheap. In the domains such as stock exchange and internet search engines, even a large unlabeled data are free and directly available.

Given labeled and unlabeled data, conventional approaches will take a choice, either supervised or unsupervised learning. When supervised learning techniques are applied, they cannot take any advantage from the unlabeled data. On the other hand, unsupervised learning methods can model a probability distribution of the training data, but they can not exploit their labels. Due to this problem some questions arise:

1. Can the additional unlabeled data help to improve performance of classifiers, when a certain amount of labeled data is given?

2. What other learning method can be used to improve classification accuracy without a lot of needed labeled data?

These issues are of high interest and as an object of current researches in the field of machine learning due to their potential in reducing the need of expensive labeled data. The first question is the main issue of the so-called *semi-supervised learning* or *labeled and unlabeled data problem* (Seeger, 2001), while the second one is the main subject of the *active learning* (Cohn *et al.*, 1994).

In this dissertation we investigate both semi-supervised learning and active learning algorithms, especially for the generative classifiers based on mixture models. The generative classifier is a classifier that built using probability densities representing classes in the data. In our case the densities are represented by using *mixture models* (McLachlan & Peel, 2000) as a linear combination of kernel densities.

1.1 Semi-Supervised Learning

The basic idea of semi-supervised learning is to take an advantage both labeled and unlabeled data by combining supervised and unsupervised learning. The motivation is that the classification error of classifiers built using additional unlabeled data may be lower than the error obtained when the classifiers are built on the basis of the labeled data alone.

In the past ten years has been emerged strong interest in this theme. An extensive review on this theme appears in (Seeger, 2001). Theoretical investigations on the value of unlabeled data for classification have been reported by some authors e.g. in (Castelli & Cover, 1996; Ratsaby & Venkatesh, 1995). They give a positive motivation that unlabeled data can improve performance of classifiers. Using a mixture of two gaussians, Castelli and Cover proved that classification error decreases exponentially with the number of labeled data and linearly with the number of unlabeled data. The result is based on assumption that the density of unlabeled data is identifiable and the training data sets are composed of a finite number of labeled data and infinite number of unlabeled data.

Some empirical results, see e.g. in (Shahshahani & Landgrebe, 1994; Baluja, 1998; Nigam *et al.*, 2000), are consistent with the theoretical result above that unlabeled data can improve performance of classifiers. However, under certain situations they also observed that the unlabeled data can not help classification, even can *degrade* performance of classifiers.

Shahshahani and Landgrebe (Shahshahani & Landgrebe, 1994) reported that unlabeled data can always help classification under assumption that the classifiers are unbiased. They performed experiments using classifiers based on gaussian mixture models for remote sensing image understanding. However, they did not define the generative models clearly and did not also investigate the generalization error as well (see also critics on this work in (Zhang & Oles, 2000; Seeger, 2001; Cozman & Cohen, 2001).

In (Nigam *et al.*, 2000) authors emphasized that the use of unlabeled data requires a *closer match* between the data and the generative models. The authors suggested mixture of multiple components of densities in order to match the models with the data distribution. Using Naive Bayes classifiers they investigated the effect of additional unlabeled data in a text classification problem. However, the authors did not attempt to completely explain their observation on the degradation phenomena.

In recent works (Cozman & Cohen, 2001; Cozman *et al.*, 2003) the degradation phenomena was intensively studied. Using generative classifiers Cozman et al. investigated theoretically and empirically structure of generative models. They concluded that unlabeled data can degrade classification performance when a classifier assumes an *incorrect* structure. They define the *correct* structure as structure of underlying distribution that generated data sets, while *incorrect* structure for any other structure. They derived a detailed analysis of performance degradation in terms of asymptotic bias (Cozman *et al.*, 2003). However, they were also aware, that it is possible that additional sources of performance degradation can be found (Cozman & Cohen, 2001).

From the literatures above we note that unlabeled data can help classification. However, it can also degrade performance under certain conditions. Their studies emphasized to take assumption of generative models into account. However, some basic questions remain unclear. In Chapter

5 of this dissertation we will consider effect of the additional unlabeled data on generalization of classifiers for different model complexity with a focus on a *overfitting* condition. We will also investigate regularization problem using *regularized weighting factors* to adjust the contribution of unlabeled data.

1.2 Active Learning

Typically, learning machines receive whatever training labeled data sets are given to them. The training data sets are gathered by sampling at *random* from an underlying distribution. The learning machines do not have power to choose the training examples. Such learning techniques are called *passive learning*.

The other strategy is known as *active learning* (Cohn *et al.*, 1994), in which learning machines attempt to improve their performance by carefully choosing the training examples for labeling. The goal of active learning is to reduce the size of training data sets to achieve certain level of performance.

Active learning is called also as query learning (Angluin, 1988). In this paradigm the learning algorithm consists of two parts: training algorithm and query algorithm. Preliminary, learning process may begin with a weak classifier that is developed with only very small number of labeled examples. In the query algorithm, a learner selectively chooses one or a few informative samples among a pool of unlabeled sample using certain criteria. The selected samples are then presented as queries to an *oracle* - a teacher who can label any points without error - to be labeled and transfered them into a training set of labeled samples and rerun learning algorithm until convergence. This processes are repeated iteratively until some convergence criteria are met, e.g. until certain training size or satisfactory performance is met.

There are some methods of active learning in literature. They can basically be distinguished into two different approaches (Roy & McCallum, 2001). The first approach attaints an optimal solution based on a statistically optimal solution. For example is active learning methods for regression problems proposed by Cohn et al. (Cohn *et al.*, 1995; Cohn, 1997). This approach needs a closed form calculation of the expected learner's variance. For classification problems, however, the closed forms are difficult to be solved, see also in (Duda *et al.*, 2000; Roy & McCallum, 2001; Maram *et al.*, 2004; Saar-Tsechansky & Provost, 2004).

The second approach attempts to achieve optimal solution by optimizing the other criteria in order to maximize expected error reduction. This approach assigns each possible query by a utility measure and selects an optimum query with respect to the utility measure. Most active learning methods use this approach, e.g. *Query by Committee* (Seung *et al.*, 1992; Freund *et al.*, 1997), active learning using Support Vector Machines (Tong & Koller, 2001b; Schohn & Cohn, 2000; Campbell *et al.*, 2000) and *uncertainty sampling* method (Lewis & Gale, 1994).

The Query by Committee (QBC) utilizes the expected information gain as an utility measure that should be maximized during query process. The expected information gain is computed using the size of *version space* (Mitchel, 1982), a subset of parameter space that consistent to the current training examples. Maximizing the expected gain is equivalent to minimizing the size of version space (Seung *et al.*, 1992). For selection potential queries they suggested the *maximum disagreement principle*, in which a query is chosen by maximizing disagreement among committee members. Active learning method proposed by Tong & Koller (Tong & Koller, 2001b) for Support Vector Machines uses also similar criterion.

The uncertainty sampling method (Lewis & Gale, 1994) do not optimize a measure (objective function) as previous methods, but chooses heuristically potential examples which are most uncertain in class membership for current classifier. The basic idea of this approach is that the best question is that for which the answer is completely uncertain, so that the information obtained by the answer is maximum. Using this criterion, classifiers will choose queries closest to the current decision boundary in which the queries are completely uncertain.

On these methods Zang & Oles (Zhang & Oles, 2000) noted that the methods are more suitable for discriminative classifiers in which their parameters are not for the purpose of generating the class members but rather for discriminating in-class members from out-of-class members. Therefore, for generative classifiers based on mixture models for which training relies on the estimation of probability densities, the estimation using such active learning methods is inaccurate. Furthermore, in this dissertation we introduce novel active learning methods by taking prior data distribution into account: the *expected likelihood-based sampling* and the *likelihood increasing sampling* method as presented in Chapter 6.

CHAPTER 2
Mixture Models and EM Algorithm

2.1 Mixture Models

Mixture models (Titterington *et al.*, 1985) are used in statistics as a convenient semi-parametric way for modelling the probability density function. Recently, mixture models is adopted by machine learning communities in a variety of application settings including density estimation, cluster analysis (McLachlan & Basford, 1988; Banfield & Raftery, 1993; Fraley & Raftery, 1998), classification (Povinelli *et al.*, 2004), images processing (Portilla *et al.*, 2003) and function approximation (Ghahramani & Jordan, 1994). Mixture models are also relevant to be applied to many aspect of neural computing, for example for estimating data distribution in the input space of radial basis function networks (Bishop, 1995).

We consider now a density estimation problem. Let $\mathcal{D}$ be a set of finite number of data points $\{\boldsymbol{x}_1, ..., \boldsymbol{x}_N\}$ drawn from a probability density function $p(\boldsymbol{x})$. Mixture models represent the probability density as a linear combination of kernel densities. The number of kernels is typically much less then the number of data points. Using M kernels $\{\phi_1(\boldsymbol{x}), ..., \phi_M(\boldsymbol{x})\}$, mixture models can be written in the form

$$p(\boldsymbol{x}) = \sum_{j=1}^{M} \pi_j \phi_j(\boldsymbol{x}). \qquad (2.1.1)$$

The coefficient π_j is called the *mixing parameter* or *mixing coefficient* and chosen to satisfy a constrain

$$0 \leq \pi_j \leq 1, \qquad \sum_{j=1}^{M} \pi_j = 1. \qquad (2.1.2)$$

The density $\phi_j(\boldsymbol{x})$ are normalized so that

$$\phi_j(\boldsymbol{x}) \geq 0, \qquad \int \phi_j(\boldsymbol{x}) d\boldsymbol{x} = 1. \qquad (2.1.3)$$

When the kernel densities belongings to the parametric family, the densities $\phi_j(\boldsymbol{x})$ have specific parametric forms and can be denoted as $p(\boldsymbol{x}|\boldsymbol{\theta}_j)$, where $\boldsymbol{\theta}_j$ is a vector of parameters in the postulated form of the densities. The mixture models therefore can be represented in the form

$$p(\boldsymbol{x}|\boldsymbol{\Psi}) = \sum_{j=1}^{M} \pi_j p(\boldsymbol{x}|\boldsymbol{\theta}_j), \qquad (2.1.4)$$

where $\boldsymbol{\Psi} \equiv (\pi_1, ..., \pi_M, \boldsymbol{\theta}_1, ..., \boldsymbol{\theta}_M)$ is a vector containing needed complete parameters to specify the mixture.

When the kernels of normal densities (gaussians) are used, the mixture models are parameterized by centers $\boldsymbol{\mu}_j$ and covariance matrices $\boldsymbol{\Sigma}_j$ of gaussians, so that $\boldsymbol{\theta}_j \equiv (\boldsymbol{\mu}_j, \boldsymbol{\Sigma}_j)$. The kernel densities can be written explicitly in the form

$$p(\boldsymbol{x}|\boldsymbol{\theta}_j) = \frac{1}{(2\pi)^{d/2}|\boldsymbol{\Sigma}_j|^{1/2}} e^{-\frac{1}{2}(\boldsymbol{x}-\mu_j)^T \Sigma_j^{-1}(\boldsymbol{x}-\mu_j)}, \qquad (2.1.5)$$

where $|\boldsymbol{\Sigma}_j|$ and $\boldsymbol{\Sigma}_j^{-1}$ are determinant and inverse of the covariance matrix respectively. The covariance $\boldsymbol{\Sigma}_j$ is a symmetric and positive definite matrix and determines the shape of densities. Using full covariance the shape of densities are hyper-ellipsoids for which the Mahalonobis distances $(\boldsymbol{x} - \boldsymbol{\mu}_j)^T \Sigma_j^{-1} (\boldsymbol{x} - \boldsymbol{\mu}_j)$ are constant.

The mixture models with full covariance matrix as (2.1.5) can give various shape to describe distribution of the data. In practice, however, it becomes unwieldy for high-dimensional data in computation of model estimate. It is caused by highly parameterized model with $\frac{1}{2}d(d+1)$ free parameters (McLachlan & Peel, 2000). Alternatively, the other forms of covariance matrix can be used, in which the number of the free parameters is reduced by imposing constraints on the form of the matrix.

Two generic covariance matrices, *spherical* and *diagonal* covariance matrices, are often applied in many practical setting. For spherical, the density function is of the form

$$p(\boldsymbol{x}|\boldsymbol{\theta}_j) = \frac{1}{(2\pi\sigma_j^2)^{d/2}} \exp\left\{ -\frac{\|\boldsymbol{x} - \boldsymbol{\mu}_j\|^2}{2\sigma_j^2} \right\}, \qquad (2.1.6)$$

where the covariance is $\Sigma_j = \sigma_j^2 \mathbf{I}$. For diagonal covariances the density function can be written as

$$p(\boldsymbol{x}|\boldsymbol{\theta}_j) = \frac{1}{(2\pi \prod_{i=1}^{d} \sigma_{j,i}^2)^{d/2}} \exp\left\{ -\sum_{i=1}^{d} \frac{(\boldsymbol{x} - \boldsymbol{\mu}_{j,i})^2}{2\sigma_{j,i}^2} \right\}, \qquad (2.1.7)$$

where $\Sigma_j = \mathrm{diag}(\sigma_{j,1}^2, ..., \sigma_{j,d}^2)$, all off-diagonal elements of covariance equal to zero. We can choose any form of covariance, since they can model an arbitrarily provided density function if the model contains enough components (McLachlan & Basford, 1988). In practice, using full covariance fewer components will be usually needed to model a given density than those model using covariance of other forms.

The other models of covariance matrices with less restrictive constrains can be obtained by using a reparameterization of the component covariances in terms of their eigenvalue decompositions as introduced by

Banfield and Raftery (Banfield & Raftery, 1993). They proposed a covariance matrix in the form

$$\boldsymbol{\Sigma}_j = \lambda_j \mathbf{D}_j \mathbf{A}_j \mathbf{D}_j^T, \qquad (2.1.8)$$

where λ_j is a scalar, $\mathbf{D}_j = (D_{j1}, ..., D_{jd})$ is the orthogonal matrix of the
eigenvectors of $\boldsymbol{\Sigma}_j$, and $\mathbf{A}_j$ is a diagonal matrix whose elements are pro-
portional to the eigenvalues of $\boldsymbol{\Sigma}_j$. Orthogonal matrix D_j determines
orientation of the principle components, while the shape of the density
contours is determined by A_j. The similar models of the covariance matrix were also proposed by some authors in (Celeux & Govaert, 1995;
Flury *et al.*, 1993).

2.2   Maximum-Likelihood

In this section we review the principle approach to find values for the model parameters given a set of training data, known as *maximum-likelihood*.
This procedure assumes that a data set is drawn independent and identi-
cally distributed (i.i.d) from a density function $p(\boldsymbol{x}|\boldsymbol{\Psi})$. Maximum likeli-
hood seeks to find the optimum values for the parameters by maximizing
a likelihood function derived from the training data set.

Likelihood is defined as probability density of the observations and
viewed as a function of parameters. Let $\mathcal{D}$ be the training data set.
Likelihood of the parameter $\boldsymbol{\Psi}$ for the given $\mathcal{D}$ can be written in the
form:

$$L(\mathcal{D}|\boldsymbol{\Psi}) = \prod_{\boldsymbol{x}_i} p(\boldsymbol{x}_i|\boldsymbol{\Psi}). \qquad (2.2.1)$$

In practice, it is often more convenient to consider the logarithm of the
likelihood

$$\mathcal{L}(\mathcal{D}|\boldsymbol{\Psi}) = \ln L(\mathcal{D}|\boldsymbol{\Psi}) = \sum_{\boldsymbol{x}_i} \ln p(\boldsymbol{x}_i|\boldsymbol{\Psi}) \qquad (2.2.2)$$

and to find a maximum of $\mathcal{L}(\mathcal{D}|\boldsymbol{\Psi})$. Accordingly, since the density function $p(\boldsymbol{x}|\boldsymbol{\Psi})$ is given by a mixture model (2.1.4), the log-likelihood can be written in the form

$$\mathcal{L}(\mathcal{D}|\boldsymbol{\Psi}) = \sum_{\boldsymbol{x}_i} \ln \sum_j \pi_j p(\boldsymbol{x}_i|\boldsymbol{\theta}_j). \tag{2.2.3}$$

2.3   EM Algorithm

For simple case, in which the data points were known to be generated from a certain component of the mixture model, the problem of determining the parameter in the mixture model would be very straightforward. In many density estimation problems with incomplete data, however, finding of maximum-likelihood is a non-linear constrained optimization problem which difficult to solve.

In this section we consider an elegant technique to solve the problem so-called the *Expectation and Maximization* (EM) algorithm (Dempster *et al.*, 1977). EM algorithm is a general technique proposed to find maximum of likelihood iteratively. The algorithm has a number advantages including naturalness at handling the probabilistic constraints of mixture problems and its guarantees of convergence to a local optimum, without the need to set learning rate and low computational overhead (Xu & Jordan, 1996). EM has also a property that make it a particularly attractive algorithm for mixture models, especially in handling of *missing variables* or *incomplete data* problems.

In the density estimation problem we should estimate a density function given a set of data. Usually, prior information of the data are unavailable. Since a mixture model is applied to estimate a density function, we don't know which component j was responsible for generating each data point. This problem therefore is regarded as an incomplete data problem. In the following we consider how the problem can be solved using EM algorithm.

We consider now random variables $z_1, ..., z_N$ that represent "labels" of mixture components corresponding to the data points $x_1, ..., x_N$. Here we introduce *indicator variables* $z_i = (z_{i1}, ..., z_{iM})^T$, where $z_{ji} \in \{0, 1\}$ is defined as follows

$$z_{ji} = \left\{ \begin{array}{ll} 1, & \text{if } x_i \text{ was generated by component } j; \\ 0, & \text{others.} \end{array} \right. \qquad (2.3.1)$$

Since the labels of mixture components in the data set are unavailable, therefore, we consider a hypothetical *complete* data set

$$\mathcal{D}_c = \{(x_1, z_1), ..., (x_N, z_N)\},$$

where $x_i \in \mathcal{D}$ and z_i are hypothetical labels. Given the hypothetical complete data set, the log-likelihood can be represented in the form

$$\mathcal{L}_c(\mathcal{D}_c | \Psi) = \sum_{x_i} \sum_{j=1}^{M} z_{ji} \ln \pi_j p(x_i | \theta_j). \qquad (2.3.2)$$

EM algorithm is an iterative method by starting from some initial values Ψ^0. Each iteration of EM consist of two steps: expectation step (E-step) and maximization step (M-step).

2.3.1   E-Step

In the E-step we compute the expectation of the log-likelihood $\mathcal{Q}(\Psi; \Psi^{(t)})$, where $\Psi^{(t)}$ is the estimated model parameter from previous iteration. In the M-step the expected log-likelihood is maximized by updating the estimated parameter. For each iteration EM guarantees the log-likelihood will monotonically increase and converge to a local maximum. The general EM algorithm is presented in Algorithm 2.

Algorithm 1 General EM algorithm

---

1. **Input:** Training data set $\mathcal{D} = \{\mathbf{x}_1, ..., \mathbf{x}_N\}$

2. **Initialize:** parameter of the likelihood $\mathbf{\Psi}^{(0)}$

3. **Do for** $t = 0, 1, 2, ...$

   (a) **E-Step:** Compute expectation of the likelihood

   $$\mathcal{Q}(\mathbf{\Psi}; \mathbf{\Psi}^{(t)}) = \mathcal{E}_{\mathbf{\Psi}^{(t)}}[\mathcal{L}(\mathbf{\Psi}; \mathcal{D})]$$

   (b) **M-Step:** Maximize the expectation by determining $\mathbf{\Psi}^*$, so that

   $$\mathcal{Q}(\mathbf{\Psi}^*; \mathbf{\Psi}^{(t)}) \geq \mathcal{Q}(\mathbf{\Psi}; \mathbf{\Psi}^{(t)})$$

4. **Break if** $|\mathcal{L}^{(t+1)} - \mathcal{L}^{(t)}| \leq \epsilon$, where ϵ is a arbitrary small constant.

For our problem the expectation of the log-likelihood can be represented by

$$\mathcal{Q}(\mathbf{\Psi}; \mathbf{\Psi}^{(t)}) = \mathcal{E}_{\mathbf{\Psi}^{(t)}}[\mathcal{L}_c(\mathbf{\Psi}|\mathcal{D}_c)], \qquad (2.3.3)$$

since a hypothetical complete data set is considered. Here subscribe $\mathbf{\Psi}^{(t)}$ is to explicitly convey that this expectation is being affected by the use of $\mathbf{\Psi}^{(t)}$ for $\mathbf{\Psi}$. Since the complete-data log-likelihood is a linear function of z_{ji} as in (2.3.2), the expected complete-data log-likelihood $\mathcal{Q}(\mathbf{\Psi}; \mathbf{\Psi}^{(t)})$ depends only on the expectation values of z_{ji} according to the current parameters $\mathbf{\Psi}^{(t)}$. Now (McLachlan & Peel, 2000)

$$\mathcal{E}_{\mathbf{\Psi}^{(t)}}[z_{ji}|\boldsymbol{x}] = P^{(t)}(j|\boldsymbol{x}), \qquad (2.3.4)$$

where

$$P^{(t)}(j|\boldsymbol{x}_i) = \frac{\pi_j^{(t)} p(\boldsymbol{x}_i|\boldsymbol{\theta}_j^{(t)})}{\sum_{k=1}^{M} \pi_k^{(t)} p(\boldsymbol{x}_i|\boldsymbol{\theta}_k^{(t)})}. \qquad (2.3.5)$$

The quantity $P^{(t)}(j|\boldsymbol{x}_i)$ is the posterior probability that represent probability that a particular component j was responsible for generating the data point $\boldsymbol{x}_i$. Using 2.3.4 the expectation of complete-data log-likelihood in (2.3.3) can be written in the form

$$\mathcal{Q}(\mathbf{\Psi}; \mathbf{\Psi}^{(t)}) = \sum_{\boldsymbol{x}_i} \sum_j P^{(t)}(j|\boldsymbol{x}_i) \ln \pi_j p(\boldsymbol{x}_i|\boldsymbol{\theta}_j). \qquad (2.3.6)$$

The expectation above is a function of the parameters π_j and $\boldsymbol{\theta}_j$, since $\pi_j^{(t)}$ and $\boldsymbol{\theta}_j^{(t)}$ are fixed values estimated in the previous iteration.

2.3.2   M-Step

In M-step, new parameter values $\mathbf{\Psi}^{(t+1)}$ are computed by maximizing the expected complete-data log-likelihood $\mathcal{Q}(\mathbf{\Psi}; \mathbf{\Psi}^{(t)})$ with respect to the parameters $\mathbf{\Psi}$. Maximization of the expected log-likelihood exist in closed form and can be carried out by differentiating it to the parameters.

The update equations can be obtained by setting the derivatives to zero

$$\nabla_{\psi_j} \mathcal{Q}(\mathbf{\Psi}; \mathbf{\Psi}^{(t)}) = \sum_{\boldsymbol{x}_i} \sum_j P^{(t)}(j|\boldsymbol{x}_i) \nabla_{\psi_j} \ln \pi_j p(\boldsymbol{x}_i|\boldsymbol{\theta}_j) = 0, \qquad (2.3.7)$$

where ψ_j is the corresponding parameters of mixture components. The log-likelihood can be maximized via the following iterative algorithm (Nabney, 2002):

$$\boldsymbol{\mu}_j^{(t+1)} = \frac{\sum_i P^{(t)}(j|\boldsymbol{x}_i)\boldsymbol{x}_i}{\sum_i P^{(t)}(j|\boldsymbol{x}_i)} \qquad (2.3.8)$$

$$\pi_j^{(t+1)} = \frac{1}{N} \sum_i P^{(t)}(j|\boldsymbol{x}_i) \qquad (2.3.9)$$

$$\mathbf{\Sigma}_j^{(t+1)} = \frac{\sum_i P^{(t)}(j|\boldsymbol{x}_i)(\boldsymbol{x}_i - \boldsymbol{\mu}_j^{(t+1)})(\boldsymbol{x}_i - \boldsymbol{\mu}_j^{(t+1)})^T}{\sum_i P^{(t)}(j|\boldsymbol{x}_i)} \qquad (2.3.10)$$

where the posterior probabilities $P^{(t)}(j|\boldsymbol{x}_i)$ are defines as in equation (2.3.5). The update equation of covariance parameters in equation (2.3.10) are in case when covariance parameters of the component densities are of the form of full covariance matrices. For spherical covariances the update equations are as follows:

$$(\sigma_j^{(t+1)})^2 = \frac{1}{d} \frac{\sum_{i=1}^{N} P^{(t)}(j|\boldsymbol{x}_i) \|\boldsymbol{x}_i - \boldsymbol{\mu}_j^{(t+1)}\|^2}{\sum_{i=1}^{N} P^{(t)}(j|\boldsymbol{x}_i)} \qquad (2.3.11)$$

and for diagonal covariances are as follows:

$$(\sigma_{a,j}^{(t+1)})^2 = \frac{\sum_{i=1}^{N} P^{(t)}(j|\boldsymbol{x}_i)((\boldsymbol{x}_i)_a - \mu_{a,j}^{(t+1)})^2}{\sum_{i=1}^{N} P^{(t)}(j|\boldsymbol{x}_i)} \qquad (2.3.12)$$

The complete EM algorithm for mixture models is presented in Algorithm 2.

Algorithm 2 EM algorithm for mixture models

---

1. **Input:** Training data set $\mathcal{D} = \{\mathbf{x}_1, ..., \mathbf{x}_N\}$

2. **Initialize:** Let $\boldsymbol{\Psi}^{(0)}$ be an initial value of the likelihood parameters

3. **Do for** $t = 0, 1, 2, ...$

    (a) **E-Step**: Compute the posterior probabilities as in (2.3.5) to evaluate expectation of the log-likelihood $\mathcal{Q}(\boldsymbol{\Psi}; \boldsymbol{\Psi}^{(t)})$ as in (2.3.6);

    (b) **M-Step**: Determine $\boldsymbol{\Psi}^{(t+1)}$ by maximizing the expected log-likelihood $\mathcal{Q}(\boldsymbol{\Psi}; \boldsymbol{\Psi}^{(t)})$ using the update equations (2.3.8), (2.3.9) and (2.3.10).

4. **Break if** $|\mathcal{L}(\boldsymbol{\Psi}^{(t+1)}) - \mathcal{L}(\boldsymbol{\Psi}^{(t)})| \leq \epsilon$, where ϵ is an arbitrary small account.

5. **Return:** $\hat{\boldsymbol{\Psi}} \leftarrow \boldsymbol{\Psi}^{(t+1)}$

CHAPTER 3

Mixture Models for Classification

In the previous chapters we focuss on the mixture models for density estimation problem, in which probability density function is estimated using a finite number of observations. In this chapter we extend now our view of mixture models to classification problems in a supervising way. In this case all of training data sets are labaled according to the class labels and mixture models are used for estimating the class-conditional densities. The classifiers are constructed using Bayes optimal decision rule on the based the estimated densities.

We start with a brief reviews of some standard definitions, then overview about general notion of classification learning problems. Thereafter, theoretical foundation of generative classifiers is given including statistical consideration on the optimal decision rule, in which the proposed classifiers based on. Furthermore, we show how mixture models can be used to construct classifier systems and how their parameters are estimated under supervised learning framework. First we consider supervised learning of the mixture models in a simple case, in which class-conditional densities are modelled only by one component of mixture. Finally, we extend notion of the simple classifier for more complex classifiers, in which class-conditional densities are modelled by multiple mixture components. To learn the classifiers, the learning algorithms are developed under EM framework. The algorithm therefore can be expanded for semi-supervised learning problems as will be considered in the next chapter.

3.1   Classification

Classification is a task to find a rule which based on observations for assigning an object to one class of a set of classes. Classification problems can be found in almost all of human activities, in everyday life such as recognizing and identifying voice of our friends also in scientific and engineering endeavors such as genomic data classification (Brown *et al.*, 2000), abnormal cells identification (Raab & Elton, 1993), handwritten character recognition (LeCun *et al.*, 1995) and documents classification (Nigam *et al.*, 2000).

In the machine learning, the problems of classification are solved by building classification systems, in which a classifier is learned by exposing it some empirical data sets as well as a sequence of examples, so that the systems can automatically classify new examples. Learning in this context is understood as *inductive inference*, in which the system observes examples that represent information so that it is capable of *generalization* to unseen examples.

Generally, there are two different approaches of classification technique: *diagnostic* approach and *sampling* approach (Ripley, 1996). The first approach includes *discriminative* methods, in which the methods directly estimate a posterior probabilities function. These methods can be found, for example in learning procedures for the neural networks and Support Vector Machines (SVMs). The second approach includes the *generative* methods, in which the classifiers are constructed using generative models such as mixture models to estimate class probability densities. Under this framework the generative models are used for classification by turning it around an optimal decision rule. Gaussian mixture models-based classifiers and Naive Bayes classifiers are examples of this methods.

3.2 Classification Learning

Generally, the classification learning refers to the supervised learning, in case the training data are labeled by discrete quantities describing classes or categories. In machine learning it is assumed that a supervisor is available and has a knowledge about an environment. In the problem of classification the environment is random vectors $x \in \mathbb{R}^d$ that will be transferred into the learning machine and supervisor. With that knowledge the supervisor is able to provide the machine with a target output z for each input vector x. Therefore, in the classification learning the learning machine is trained from a training data set $\mathcal{D}$ that consists of pairs (x_i, z_i) of input vector x_i and target output z_i,

$$\mathcal{D} = \{(x_1, z_1), ..., (x_n, z_n)\}.$$

The target outputs $z_i \in \mathcal{C}$ are discrete quantities describing class labels or categories for each input vector x_i.

The learning process can be described through a model (Vapnik, 1998) as illustrated in Figure 3.1. The learning model represents a learning system using three interrelated components: (i) generator of the data set; (ii) supervisor; and (iii) learning machine. The generator determines an environment of the learning machine and the supervisor. It generates input vectors $x \in \mathbb{R}^d$ according to a fixed but unknown probability distribution function $p(\boldsymbol{x})$. The supervisor provides a desired output $\boldsymbol{z}$ for each input vectors $\boldsymbol{x}$ received from the environment, in accordance with the conditional distribution function $p(\boldsymbol{x}|\boldsymbol{z})$. The learning machine observes the training data set of pairs $(\boldsymbol{x}_1, \boldsymbol{z}_1), ..., (\boldsymbol{x}_N, \boldsymbol{z}_N)$ which contain N input vectors $\boldsymbol{x}$ and output values $\boldsymbol{z}$ returned by the supervisor. During learning process the learning machine gives actions in the form of a set of functions. Furthermore, this model considers the learning problems as selecting an appropriate function that can give an approximation of supervisor's response for each input data in an optimal fashion.

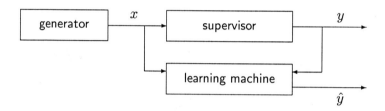

Figure 3.1: Model learning from examples (Vapnik, 1998).

Let $\phi(\boldsymbol{x}, \alpha), \alpha \in \Lambda$, be a decision function of the learning machine for an input vector $\boldsymbol{x}$ and $\Lambda = \{\alpha_1, ..., \alpha_a\}$ be a set of admissible actions. The supervised learning therefore can be described as an approximation problem. That means during learning process the learning machine attempts to find an appropriate function $\phi(\boldsymbol{x}, \alpha^*), \alpha^* \in \Lambda$, which on the basis training data set resulting the best approximate of target values returned by the supervisor.

Now we consider a classification problem in which the training data set consist of c classes, $\mathcal{C} = \{C_1, ..., C_c\}$. For given input vector $\boldsymbol{x}$, the action of the learning machine and the response of supervisor take one of the class labels in $\mathcal{C}$. To classify an input vector $\boldsymbol{x}$, the general approach is by using the posterior probability of class membership $P(C_k|\boldsymbol{x})$, which gives the probability that the class is C_k for input vector $\boldsymbol{x}$.

Furthermore, it is necessary to find an optimal decision rule in order to assign a class label for every input vector with minimum probability of misclassification. In order to achieve the optimal decision, the usual way is by defining a *loss function* $L(\boldsymbol{z}, \phi(\boldsymbol{x}, \alpha))$ that exactly measures the loss of each action incurred when the decision provided by the learning machine is $\phi(\boldsymbol{x}, \alpha)$ and the response of the supervisor for given input vector is $\boldsymbol{z}$. The loss function takes a finite number of values. The simplest loss function is the *one-zero* loss function that assigns a unit loss to any error

$$L(\boldsymbol{z}|\phi(\boldsymbol{x}, \alpha)) = \begin{cases} 0, & \text{if } \boldsymbol{z} = \phi(\boldsymbol{x}, \alpha) \\ 1, & \text{if } \boldsymbol{z} \neq \phi(\boldsymbol{x}, \alpha) \end{cases} \qquad (3.2.1)$$

Here, α is the action of machine and $\boldsymbol{z}$ is the response of the supervisor (the true output) for the given input vector $\boldsymbol{x}$.

Suppose $\phi(\boldsymbol{x}, \alpha_i)$ is a particular decision of the learning machine associated with an action α_i of the machine for an input vector $\boldsymbol{x}$. This decision will incur the loss $L(C_k, \phi(\boldsymbol{x}, \alpha_i))$ when the response of supervisor (true class label) is C_k. For a classification problem of c classes, the expected risk associated with the particular decision $\phi(\boldsymbol{x}, \alpha_i)$ is expressed by the *conditional risk* as follows

$$R(\alpha_i|\boldsymbol{x}) = \sum_{k=1}^{c} L(\phi(\boldsymbol{x}, \alpha_i), C_k) P(C_k|\boldsymbol{x}), \qquad (3.2.2)$$

where $\phi(\boldsymbol{x}, \alpha_i)$ is a decision function returned by the machine and takes value one of c classes. Let $\alpha(\boldsymbol{x})$ be action of the learning machine for an input vector $\boldsymbol{x}$. The total expected value of the loss is given by the *total risk* in the form

$$R = \int R(\alpha(\boldsymbol{x})|\boldsymbol{x})\, p(\boldsymbol{x}) dx, \qquad (3.2.3)$$

where $p(\boldsymbol{x})$ is the probability density function generating the data set. Here, the integral is taken over entire input vector space. The total risk defines the criterion of quality of the chosen decision. The optimal decision rule then can be made by minimizing the total risk.

3.3   Optimal Decision Rule

For the loss function $L(C_k, \phi(\boldsymbol{x}, \alpha_i))$ defined in (3.2.1), the risk R as in (3.2.3) determines the probability of different output upon the output given by the supervisor and the learning machine. The different outputs in this case are called a *classification error* or an *error rate*. The problem of classification is therefore to minimize the classification error on the set of decision function $\phi(\boldsymbol{x}, \alpha), \alpha \in \Lambda$ when the training data is available but the joint probability function $p(\boldsymbol{x}, \boldsymbol{z})$ is unknown.

From equation (3.2.3) the minimum value of the total risk can be achieved if the action of machine α_i for every input vector $\boldsymbol{x}$ minimizes the conditional risk $R(\alpha_i|\boldsymbol{x})$. In order to minimize the risk, the *optimal Bayes decision rule* suggests that an action $\alpha^* \in \Lambda$ given by the admissible actions is selected for which the conditional risk for given input vector $\boldsymbol{x}$ is minimum. Thus the probability of misclassification can be minimized by selecting a class or a category that maximizes the *posterior probability* $P(C_k|\boldsymbol{x})$. This Bayes decision rule is an optimal decision to achieve the best performance. This rule is called also the *maximum a posteriori* (MAP) rule, where an input vector $\boldsymbol{x}$ is assigned to a class C_k having the largest posterior probability

$$P(C_k|\boldsymbol{x}) > P(C_j|\boldsymbol{x}) \text{ for all } j \neq k. \tag{3.3.1}$$

This optimal decision rule is essential for all classifier systems in decision making of classification.

3.4 Model-Based Classifiers

The optimal Bayes decision rule can be used to design classifier systems. Let $\phi(\boldsymbol{x})$ be a classifier mapping input space $\mathcal{X}$ to the discrete output space $\mathcal{C}$,

$$\phi(\boldsymbol{x}) : \mathcal{X} \rightarrow \mathcal{C}.$$

For the one-zero loss function the classifier can be expressed in the form

$$\phi(\boldsymbol{x}) = \arg\max_{C_k} P(C_k|\boldsymbol{x}), \tag{3.4.1}$$

where $P(C_k|\boldsymbol{x})$ is the posterior probability of class membership.

In a statistical framework of pattern recognition, the posterior probabilities can be related to terms of the *class-conditional probabilities* $p(\boldsymbol{x}|C_k)$ and the *prior* probabilities $P(C_k)$ through the *Bayes's theorem* as follows (Bishop, 1995)

$$P(C_k|\boldsymbol{x}) = \frac{P(C_k)p(\boldsymbol{x}|C_k)}{p(\boldsymbol{x})}. \tag{3.4.2}$$

The denominator of the theorem $p(\boldsymbol{x})$ is the unconditional probability and expressed in the form

$$p(\boldsymbol{x}) = \sum_{k=1}^{c} P(C_k)p(\boldsymbol{x}|C_k). \tag{3.4.3}$$

The unconditional probability $p(\boldsymbol{x})$ ensures that the posterior probabilities sum to unity

$$\sum_{k=1}^{c} P(C_k|\boldsymbol{x}) = 1. \tag{3.4.4}$$

In most situations, however, the class-conditional densities are usually unknown but a finite number of labeled data is available. In this case, techniques of the density estimation such as mixture models are useful in estimating the probabilities. Indeed, performance of a classifier is determined by estimated generative model. Therefore, classification learning for model-based classifiers can be regarded as a process of recovering the generative models.

3.5   Supervised Learning of Mixture Models

In the generative approach, classifiers are constructed from the class-conditional densities estimated using a set of training data. The densities can be estimated using density estimators such as mixture models. In this section we consider supervised learning of mixture models to construct classifier systems under EM framework. First we consider simplest model, in which class-conditional densities are modelled only by one component of mixture. The similar notion is then extended for more complex classifiers, in which class-conditional densities are represented by multiple mixture components.

3.5.1   Learning of Simple Models

In classification problems, learning machines are given a set of labeled training examples

$$\mathcal{D} = \{(\boldsymbol{x}_1, \boldsymbol{z}_1), ..., (\boldsymbol{x}_\ell, \boldsymbol{z}_\ell)\},$$

where $\boldsymbol{z}_i$ are class labels of input vectors $\boldsymbol{x}_i$. We consider a simplest problem in which each class of the data is regarded to be generated exactly from one probability density. To estimate the class-conditional densities we can build a mixture model of several components, each one represents a class.

Suppose the data set consist of c classes $\mathcal{C} = \{C_1, ..., C_c\}$ and $\boldsymbol{z}_i \in \mathcal{C}$. Since one component of the mixture associates with a class of data set, then there are one-to-one correspondence between the mixture components and the classes. We can therefore build a mixture of c component densities, each component represents different class density. The mixture model can be written in the form

$$p(x|\boldsymbol{\Psi}) = \sum_k \pi_k p(\boldsymbol{x}|\boldsymbol{\theta}_k), \qquad (3.5.1)$$

In this case, indices of the mixture components associate with the different classes, so that component density $p(\boldsymbol{x}|\boldsymbol{\theta}_k)$ represents the class-conditional density $p(\boldsymbol{x}|C_k)$ and the mixing parameter π_k represents the *prior* probability of class C_k.

Here, there are not missing values since all training data are labeled by class labels associated to the component of mixture. For each data points are known which component of the mixture was responsible to generate it. The log-likelihood of the model therefore can be simply written in the form

$$\mathcal{L}(\boldsymbol{\Psi}; \mathcal{D}) = \sum_k \sum_{\boldsymbol{x} \in \mathcal{D}_k} \ln \pi_k p(\boldsymbol{x}|\boldsymbol{\theta}_k), \qquad (3.5.2)$$

where $\mathcal{D}_k$ is sub-set of the training data set $\mathcal{D}$ belongs to class C_k.

The class labels can be denoted as a vector $\boldsymbol{z}_i = (z_{i1}, ..., z_{ic})^T$ with binary elements, $z_{ki} \in \{1, 0\}$ as defined in (2.3.1). Using the notation we can write the log-likelihood (3.5.2) in the form

$$\mathcal{L}(\boldsymbol{\Psi}; \mathcal{D}) = \sum_i \sum_k z_{ki} \ln \pi_k p(\boldsymbol{x}_i|\boldsymbol{\theta}_k). \qquad (3.5.3)$$

The equation (3.5.3) represents the log-likelihood of *complete data*, since there is no missing values in the considered training data. Each training data point is exactly labeled by a mixture component was generated it.

The mixture parameters therefore can be computed by differentiating the log-likelihood function respect to the parameters then setting the derivatives to be zero

$$\nabla_{\boldsymbol{\Psi}} \mathcal{L}(\boldsymbol{\Psi}; \mathcal{D}) = \sum_{\boldsymbol{x}_i} \nabla_{\boldsymbol{\Psi}} \ln p(\boldsymbol{x}_i|\boldsymbol{\Psi}) = 0. \qquad (3.5.4)$$

3.5.2   Learning of Complex Models

In practice usually simple models can not cover complex data sets, in which the group structure of the data can not be modelled entirely using single component per class. In this section we consider more complex models allowing us to create quadratic or more complex decision boundaries, so that an optimal classifier can be attained. Moreover, a classifier built using the complex models will be more powerful in terms of its ability to discriminate among various class of different shapes.

We assume that a number components of a mixture model have generated a class of the data. The other information about generating data, however, are not available. In this case, the data can be regarded *incomplete*, since only class labels of the data set are available but information about which components of the mixture generated the certain class of the data are not available. To handle this problem, there are two different scenarios. First, for each class-conditional density we construct a mixture model, see e.g. in (Nabney, 2002). The other scenario is by constructing a mixture model and train it with some constraints and regularization. In this section we present learning algorithm of the mixture models for the last scenario, in which a mixture model is constructed to estimate conditional densities of all considered classes. This method is inspired by work of Nigam et al. (Nigam *et al.*, 2000) for Naive Bayes classifiers.

In Chapter 2 we showed how to estimate parameters of mixture models using the maximum-likelihood approach given a set of *unlabeled* data. For our case now the model parameters can be found in a similar way by considering our problem as an incomplete data problem by introducing other missing values, additional constrains and regularization. The missing values mentioned here are not only the *component labels* of data points but also the class labels of mixture components. Again, we apply EM algorithm to handle this problem.

Suppose a finite number of labeled data from c classes is given,

$$\mathcal{D} = (\boldsymbol{x}_1, \boldsymbol{z}_1), ..., (\boldsymbol{x}_\ell, \boldsymbol{z}_\ell),$$

where $\boldsymbol{x}_i \in \mathbb{R}^d$, ℓ is the number of the data points and $\boldsymbol{z}_i \in \{C_1, ..., C_c\}$ is a class label corresponding to an input example $\boldsymbol{x}_i$. Similar as in (2.3.1), we denote a class label as a vector $\boldsymbol{z}_i = (z_{i1}, ..., z_{ic})^T$ consisting of elements are defined as follows

$$z_{ki} = \begin{cases} 1, & \text{if } \boldsymbol{x}_i \text{ belongs to class } C_k; \\ 0, & \text{others.} \end{cases} \tag{3.5.5}$$

We consider now a mixture model that consist of M mixture components

$$p(\boldsymbol{x}|\boldsymbol{\Psi}) = \sum_{j=1}^{M} \pi_j p(\boldsymbol{x}|\boldsymbol{\theta}_j) \tag{3.5.6}$$

to estimate c class-conditional densities. Indeed, in this case the number component of mixture is more than the number of classes, $M > c$. Here, π_j and $p(\boldsymbol{x}_i|\boldsymbol{\theta}_j)$ are the mixing coefficients of mixture and the conditional probability densities of component j respectively. Since there are not one-to-one correspondence between mixture components and classes, we separate the class labels and the labels of mixture components tag the data.

We restrict our discuss only on a two-classes classification problem, so that $c = 2$, and the class labels of mixture components are available. Let $G_k = \{j|j \in C_k\}$ be a set of mixture components belongs to the class C_k. To label each mixture j component we introduce a indicator variable $\boldsymbol{t}_j$. The variable is represented as a vector $\boldsymbol{t}_j = (t_{j1}, ..., t_{jc})^T$ with elements t_{kj} are defined as follows

$$t_{kj} = \begin{cases} 1, & \text{if component } j \text{ belongs to class } C_k; \\ 0, & \text{others.} \end{cases} \tag{3.5.7}$$

We can therefore label each component of mixture according to which class of it belong to. We consider now a set of pairs

$$\mathcal{T} = \{(j, \boldsymbol{t}_j)|j = 1, ..., M\}$$

represents correspondence among mixture components j and their class labels $\boldsymbol{t}_j$.

Using the class labels of components $\boldsymbol{t}_j$, the class-conditional densities of class C_k can be represented in the form

$$P(x\|C_k) = \sum_{j \in G_k} \pi_j p(x|\boldsymbol{\theta}_j) \qquad (3.5.8)$$

$P(\cdot\|\cdot)$ denotes the class-conditional densities approximated using a part of mixture components as in (5.2.14). Using indicator variables (5.2.15) the class-conditional densities (3.5.8) can be also written in the form

$$P(x\|C_k) = \sum_{j} t_{kj} \pi_j p(x|\boldsymbol{\theta}_j) \qquad (3.5.9)$$

and the prior probabilities in the form

$$P(C_k) = \sum_{j \in G_k} \pi_j = \sum_{j} t_{kj} \pi_j. \qquad (3.5.10)$$

Here G_k is a set of mixture components belongs to class C_k.

Learning Algorithm

In Chapter 2 we showed how to estimate parameters of mixture models using the maximum-likelihood given a set of unlabeled data. For our case now the parameters can be found in a similar way by considering the problem as an incomplete data problem with some additional constrains.

Since the component labels for every data point are unavailable, we consider a hypothetical complete data set, in which each data point is labeled with a label of component which generated it. We introduce a set of variables

$$\{\boldsymbol{y}_1, \boldsymbol{y}_2, ..., \boldsymbol{y}_\ell\}$$

corresponding to the data points $\{\boldsymbol{x}_1, ..., \boldsymbol{x}_\ell\}$, where $\boldsymbol{y}_i = (y_{i1}, ..., y_{iM})^T$ with elements $y_{ji} \in \{1, 0\}$ represents whether a data point $\boldsymbol{x}_i$ is regarded or not regarded generated from component j of the mixture as defined in (2.3.1). The hypothetical complete data, therefore, can be expressed as follows

$$\mathcal{D}^c = \{(\boldsymbol{x}_1, \boldsymbol{y}_1), ..., (\boldsymbol{x}_\ell, \boldsymbol{y}_\ell)\} \tag{3.5.11}$$

and the corresponding complete-data log-likelihood can be written in the form

$$\mathcal{L}^c(\boldsymbol{\Psi}; \mathcal{D}^c) = \sum_i \sum_j y_{ji} \ln \pi_j p(\boldsymbol{x}_i|\boldsymbol{\theta}_j). \tag{3.5.12}$$

E-Step

We consider now EM algorithm to approximate parameters of the mixture models under constrains above. In the expectation (E)-step of EM we compute the expectation of the complete-data log-likelihood $\mathcal{Q}(\boldsymbol{\Psi}; \boldsymbol{\Psi}^{(t)})$ as follows

$$\mathcal{Q}(\boldsymbol{\Psi}; \boldsymbol{\Psi}^{(t)}) = \mathcal{E}_{\boldsymbol{\Psi}^{(t)}}[\mathcal{L}^c(\boldsymbol{\Psi}; \mathcal{D}^c)], \tag{3.5.13}$$

where $\boldsymbol{\Psi}^{(t)}$ is the parameter estimates from previous iteration. Since the complete-data log-likelihood (3.5.12) is a linear function of the component labels of the data points y_{ji}, the expected complete-data log-likelihood (3.5.13) depends only on the expectation values $\mathcal{E}[y_{ji}]$ that are given by the following posterior probabilities (McLachlan & Peel, 2000)

$$P(j|\boldsymbol{x}_i) = \frac{\pi_j p_j(\boldsymbol{x}_i|\boldsymbol{\theta}_j)}{\sum_j \pi_j p_j(\boldsymbol{x}_i|\boldsymbol{\theta}_j)}. \tag{3.5.14}$$

Due to the constrain that the components of mixture were partitioned into some different classes, it is not allowed to use the posterior probabilities $P(j|\boldsymbol{x}_i)$ directly for computing the expectation of complete-data log-likelihood (3.5.13). We must restrict therefore that data points $\boldsymbol{x}_i$ from a class $\mathcal{C}_k$ have to be generated only by components of mixture from the same class, $\boldsymbol{t}_j \in \mathcal{C}_k$. In other word the constrain $\boldsymbol{z}_i = \boldsymbol{t}_j$ must be satisfied. Therefore we introduce the *restricted* component membership $\tau(j|\boldsymbol{x})$ in the form

$$\tau(j|\boldsymbol{x}_i) = \frac{\delta_{\boldsymbol{t}_j,\boldsymbol{z}_i} P(j|\boldsymbol{x}_i)}{\sum_j \delta_{\boldsymbol{t}_j,\boldsymbol{z}_i} P(j|\boldsymbol{x}_i)}, \tag{3.5.15}$$

where

$$\delta_{\boldsymbol{t}_j,\boldsymbol{z}_i} = \begin{cases} 1, & \text{if } \boldsymbol{t}_j = \boldsymbol{z}_i; \\ 0, & \text{if } \boldsymbol{t}_j \neq \boldsymbol{z}_i \end{cases} \tag{3.5.16}$$

The denominator of (3.5.15) is to ensure the sum to unity

$$\sum_{j=1}^{M} \tau(j|\boldsymbol{x}) = 1. \tag{3.5.17}$$

In view of the constrain above the expectation of complete-data log-likelihood should be computed using the restricted component membership (3.5.15)

$$\mathcal{Q}(\boldsymbol{\Psi}; \boldsymbol{\Psi}^{(t)}) = \sum_{\boldsymbol{x}_i \in \mathcal{D}} \sum_j \tau^{(t)}(j|\boldsymbol{x}_i) \ln \pi_j p(\boldsymbol{x}_i|\boldsymbol{\theta}_j). \tag{3.5.18}$$

Since the values of $\pi_j^{(t)}$ and $\boldsymbol{\theta}_j^{(t)}$ to compute $\tau^{(t)}(j|\boldsymbol{x}_i)$ are fixed, the expectation $\mathcal{Q}(\boldsymbol{\Psi}; \boldsymbol{\Psi}^{(t)})$ is a function of the parameters π_j and $\boldsymbol{\theta}_j$. Hence, in expectation-step of EM we should compute the restricted component memberships $\tau^{(t)}(j|\boldsymbol{x}_i)$ using previous computed parameters $\boldsymbol{\Psi}^{(t)}$.

M-Step

Thereafter, in maximization step of EM the parameters of mixtures $\boldsymbol{\Psi}^{(t+1)}$ are estimated by maximizing the expectation of complete-data log-likelihood (3.5.18). Update equations for estimation of the mixture parameters can be found by performing differentiation of the expected complete-data log-likelihood respect to the parameters

$$\nabla_{\psi_j} \mathcal{Q}(\mathbf{\Psi}; \mathbf{\Psi}^{(t)}) = \sum_{\boldsymbol{x}_i \in \mathcal{D}} \sum_j \tau^{(t)}(j|\boldsymbol{x}_i) \nabla_{\psi_j} \ln[\pi_j p_j(\boldsymbol{x}_i|\boldsymbol{\theta}_j)] \qquad (3.5.19)$$

and setting the derivatives to zero

$$\nabla_{\psi_j} \mathcal{Q}(\mathbf{\Psi}; \mathbf{\Psi}^{(t)}) = 0, \qquad (3.5.20)$$

where ψ_j is the corresponding parameters of the mixture components.

For component densities of gaussians with mean and covariance parameters are $\boldsymbol{\mu}_j$ and $\boldsymbol{\Sigma}_j$ respectively, the update equations of the mixture parameters can be obtained in the form

$$\boldsymbol{\mu}_j^{(t+1)} = \frac{\sum_{\boldsymbol{x}_i \in \mathcal{D}} \boldsymbol{x}_i \tau^{(t)}(j|\boldsymbol{x}_i)}{\sum_i \tau^{(t)}(j|\boldsymbol{x}_i)} \qquad (3.5.21)$$

$$\pi_j^{(t+1)} = \frac{1}{\ell} \sum_{\boldsymbol{x}_i \in \mathcal{D}} \tau^{(t)}(j|\boldsymbol{x}_i) \qquad (3.5.22)$$

$$\boldsymbol{\Sigma}_j^{(t+1)} = \frac{\sum_{\boldsymbol{x}_i \in \mathcal{D}} \tau^{(t)}(j|\boldsymbol{x}_i)(\boldsymbol{x}_i - \boldsymbol{\mu}_j^{(t+1)})(\boldsymbol{x}_i - \boldsymbol{\mu}_j^{(t+1)})^T}{\sum_{\boldsymbol{x}_i \in \mathcal{D}} \tau^{(t)}(j|\boldsymbol{x}_i)} \quad (3.5.23)$$

The complete EM algorithm for this case is presented in Algorithm 3.

Algorithm 3 EM algorithm of the mixture models for multiple components per class

---

1. **Input:** Labeled training set $\mathcal{D} = \{(\mathbf{x}_i, \mathbf{z}_i), ..., (\mathbf{x}_\ell, \mathbf{z}_\ell)\}$, number of mixture component M, class labels of mixture component $\{\mathbf{t}_j | j = 1, ..., M\}$.

2. **Initialize:** Model parameters $\mathbf{\Psi}^{(0)}$, posterior probabilities $P^{(0)}(j|\mathbf{x})$.

3. **Do for** $t = 0, ..., t_m$

   (a) E-Step: Compute the expectation of log-likelihood $\mathcal{Q}(\mathbf{\Psi}; \mathbf{\Psi}^{(t)})$ as in (3.5.18) by evaluating the restricted component memberships $\tau^{(t+1)}(j|\mathbf{x}_i)$ as follows

      i. Compute the component memberships using $\mathbf{\Psi}^{(t)}$:

$$P(j|\mathbf{x}_i)^{(t+1)} = \frac{\pi_j^{(t)} p_j(\mathbf{x}_i|\boldsymbol{\theta}_j^{(t)})}{\sum_j \pi_j^{(t)} p_j(\mathbf{x}_i|\boldsymbol{\theta}_j^{(t)})}$$

      ii. Evaluate the restricted component memberships

$$\tau^{(t+1)}(j|\mathbf{x}_i) = \frac{\delta_{\mathbf{t}_j, \mathbf{z}_i} P^{(t+1)}(j|\mathbf{x}_i)}{\sum_j \delta_{\mathbf{t}_j, \mathbf{z}_i} P^{(t+1)}(j|\mathbf{x}_i)}$$

   (b) M-Step: Maximize the expectation of log-likelihood by estimating $\mathbf{\Psi}^{(t+1)}$ given $\tau^{(t+1)}(j|\mathbf{x}_i)$ using upgrade equations (3.5.21), (3.5.22), and (3.5.23) for gaussian mixtures.

4. **Break if** $|\Delta\mathcal{L}| \leq \epsilon$, ϵ is an arbitrary small constant.

5. **Output:** Parameter estimate $\mathbf{\Psi}$.

CHAPTER 4

LBGU-EM Algorithm for Density Estimation

In the previous chapter we considered the mixture models for density estimation. An important special case is the gaussian mixture model where each component is a gaussian distribution and all components are combined using mixing parameters which form a partition of unity. The standard method for determining the optimal parameter values for the Gaussians and the mixing components is the EM algorithm (Dempster *et al.*, 1977). EM starts from the given initial parameter values and modifies them iteratively such that the likelihood of the data is increased in every iteration. EM is a local optimization method and very sensitive to initialization (Ormoneit & Tresp, 1998; Meila & Heckerman, 1998; Usama Fayyad & Bradley, 1998; Xu & Jordan, 1996).

To overcome this initialization dependence problem, the K-means algorithm is often used to determine initial positions for the gaussian mixture components: after random initialization K-means is run until convergence and thereafter the actual EM algorithm starts from the positions determined by K-means. However, since K-means is itself a local method (actually it can be seen as efficiently computable special case of EM in the limit of vanishing gaussian variance) the strong dependence on initialization persist.

In this chapter a novel method for mixture density estimation will be presented. This chapter is based on (Iswanto & Fritzke, 2002) in which we studied the initialization problem of EM empirically and investigate a possibility to remedy the problem by using the LBG-U algorithm (Fritzke, 1997). The LBG-U algorithm is a generalization of the LBG method (Linde *et al.*, 1980). In contrast to LBG, LBG-U shows only a weak dependence on initialization and generates in many cases codebooks with considerably lower quantization error as reported in (Fritzke, 1997).

Nevertheless it is not at all self-understood that LBG-U is also a good initialization method of EM for gaussian mixture models, since the objective function (the log-likelihood of the data) is different from that used by LBG and LBG-U (the mean square quantization error). Experiments with EM using different initializations (LBG, LBG-U and random initialization) have been performed on several data sets with different dimensionality. The results indicate, that LBG-U can indeed be very useful as initialization method for EM.

4.1   Initialization of EM

EM starts from the given initial parameter values and modifies them iteratively, such that the log-likelihood given the training data set is increased in every step. The algorithm is known to be convergence to a local maximum (Dempster *et al.*, 1977; Redner & Walker, 1984) and very sensitive to initialization (Ormoneit & Tresp, 1998; Meila & Heckerman, 1998; Usama Fayyad & Bradley, 1998; Xu & Jordan, 1996). When the initial values are far from the convergent value, or starting points do not separate the group means sufficiently, the step size $\Delta \mathcal{L}$ is particularly large in many practical implementations. Even EM often moves the iterates quickly and being trapped in a poor local maxima. The other problem in empirical results as reported in (Redner & Walker, 1984), EM demonstrates slow convergence on a gaussian mixture model problem for which the mixture components were not well separated. To avoid the initialization problem, the most obvious approach is to use the good initial estimates of mixture parameters to compute the initial component membership $P(j|\boldsymbol{x}_i)$. In practice this approach can also accelerate convergence.

The common procedure of the initialization is to partition the training data set into M clusters and fit components of mixture to the data points falling in each partition. We assign the partitions as *Voronoi* regions, in which the points belong to the nearest cluster center. The set of points falling in a Voronoi region j is called as Voronoi set of the region and denoted as $\mathcal{V}_j$. Typically the partition techniques produce clusters by optimizing a criterion function. The frequently used criterion is the mean squared error as follows

$$E(\mathcal{D}, \mathcal{A}) = \frac{1}{N} \sum_{c \in \mathcal{A}} \sum_{\boldsymbol{x} \in \mathcal{V}_c} \|\boldsymbol{x} - \boldsymbol{\mu}_c\|^2. \qquad (4.1.1)$$

Here, $\mathcal{A} = \{c_1, .., c_M\}$ is set of clusters, $\boldsymbol{\mu}_c$ is a mean vector representing cluster c. The algorithm such as K-means and LBG are the common algorithms that used for data partitioning purposes.

In practice finding a good maximum of the log-likelihood is difficult and maximization of the log-likelihood function is non-trivial (Scott, 1992). There are a wide range of fits from different initializations. The EM algorithm as introduced above starts with some initial values at the maximum likelihood parameters, $\boldsymbol{\Psi}^{(0)}$, and then proceeds to generate successive estimations, $\Psi^{(1)}, \Psi^{(2)}, \ldots \Psi^{(t)}$, iteratively by repeating the E-step and M-step. Each EM iteration increases the log-likelihood and is guaranteed toward convergence to a local maximum. Only data points with large posterior probabilities for a given kernel do affect the new parameters. This is the local aspect of EM that makes EM sensitive to initial parameter values and leads to high variance of the results. The methods to initialize EM such as K-means solutions was found that for EM showed only small improvement over random initialization (Meila & Heckerman, 1998). Since K-means is itself is a local method, its strong dependence on initialization persist.

In the following we investigate a possibility to remedy the initialization problem by using the LBG-U algorithm (Fritzke, 1997) to refine the initial points to a point likely to be closer to the cluster centers. The challenge is to perform refinement efficiently. The LBG-U is a generalization of the LBG algorithm (Linde *et al.*, 1980). LBG is similar as K-means and sensitive to initialization. In contrast to LBG, LBG-U has shown only a weak dependence on initialization and generates in many cases codebooks with considerably lower quantization error (Fritzke, 1997). The codebooks can never be worse than those generated by LBG, since the initial iteration of LBG-U is LBG.

4.2   LBG-U Algorithm

The LBG-U is an improvement of LBG algorithm for vector quantization. The underlying problem in vector quantization is to construct a *codebook*, a set of reference vectors $\{\mathbf{w}_c | c \in \mathcal{A}\}$, where $\mathcal{A} = \{c_1, \ldots, c_M\}$ is a set of units which minimizes the quantization error. The quantization error is given in the form

$$E(\mathcal{D}, \mathcal{A}) = \frac{1}{|\mathcal{D}|} \sum_{c \in \mathcal{A}} \sum_{x \in \mathcal{V}_c} \|\boldsymbol{x} - \mathbf{w}_c\|^2, \qquad (4.2.1)$$

where $\mathcal{V}_c$ is Voronoi set of unit c, namely a set of data vectors for which a particular codebook vector $\mathbf{w}_c$ is nearest.

The learning algorithm of LBG involve an iteration of the following two steps, called *Llyod* iteration, in its inner loop: computation of the Voronoi sets $\mathcal{V}_c$ and moving of the reference vectors $\mathbf{w}_c$ to the centroid of its Voronoi region

$$\mathbf{w}_c = \frac{1}{|\mathcal{V}_c|} \sum_{x \in \mathcal{V}_c} x. \qquad (4.2.2)$$

The theoretical foundation for LBG is that a necessary condition for a set of reference vectors to minimize the quantization error. Equation (4.2.2) holds for all reference vectors.

Algorithm 4 LBG algorithm (Linde *et al.*, 1980)

---

1. **Input:** Data set $\mathcal{D} = \{\mathbf{x}_1, ..., \mathbf{x}_N\}$ and a set of units $\mathcal{A} = \{c_1, ..., c_M\}$.

2. **Initialize:** The reference vector of all units $\{\mathbf{w}_c | c \in \mathcal{A}\}$ are sampled at random from the data set.

3. **Do** $t = 0, 1, 2, ...$

   (a) Evaluate for each unit its Voronoi set $\{\mathcal{V}_c | c \in \mathcal{A}^{(t)}\}$.

   (b) Move the reference vector of each unit to the centroid of its Voronoi set

4. **Break if** Error quantization $E^{(t+1)} \not< E^{(t)}$

5. **Return:** The reference vectors $\{\mathbf{w}_c | c \in \mathcal{A}\}$.

The LBG-U consists of repeated runs of LBG. Each time LBG has converged, a particular measure of utility

$$\mathcal{U}(c) = E(\mathcal{D}, \mathcal{A} \backslash c) - E(\mathcal{D}, \mathcal{A}) \qquad (4.2.3)$$

and a local distortion error

$$E(c) = \sum_{x \in \mathcal{V}_c} \|x - \mathbf{w}_c\|^2 \qquad (4.2.4)$$

is assigned to each codebook vector. The utility indicates how important $\mathbf{w}_c$ is for error reduction. Thereafter, the vector with minimum utility is moved to a Voronoi region of a vector with maximum local distortion error. LBG runs again on the resulting modified codebook until convergence is reached. Another vector is moved, and so on. LBG-U (as LBG) is guaranteed converge in a finite number of iterations. In practice usually a small number of iterations is sufficient. The complete LBG-U algorithm is given in Algorithm 5.

Algorithm 5 LBG-U algorithm (Fritzke, 1997)

---

1. **Input:** Data set $\mathcal{D} = \{\mathbf{x}_1, ..., \mathbf{x}_N\}$ and a set of unit $\mathcal{A} = \{c_1, ..., c_M\}$.

2. **Initialize:** The reference vector of all units $\{\mathbf{w}_c | c \in \mathcal{A}\}$ are sampled at random from the data set, compute error $E_{LBGU} := E(\mathcal{D}, \mathcal{A})$, stop := FALSE

3. **While** stop := FALSE

   (a) Run LBG until convergence and compute the error $E_{LBG} =: E(\mathcal{D}, \mathcal{A})$

   (b) **If** $E_{LBG} \geq E_{LBGU}$ stop := TRUE

   (c) **Else**

      i. Set $E_{LBGU} := E_{LBG}$ and save codebook $\mathcal{K}_{LBGU} := \{\mathbf{w}_c | c \in \mathcal{A}\}$

      ii. determine unit with minimum utility: $c_a := \arg\min_{c \in \mathcal{A}} U(c)$

      iii. determine unit with maximum error: $c_b := \arg\max_{c \in \mathcal{A}} E(c)$

      iv. move $\mathbf{w}_a$ beside $\mathbf{w}_b$, e.g. $\mathbf{w}_a := \mathbf{w}_b + \hat{\mathbf{u}}\epsilon\sqrt{E(c_b)/|\mathcal{D}|}$, where ϵ is a small constant and $\hat{\mathbf{u}}$ is a random vector from d-dimensional unit sphere.

4. **Return:** The current set of codebook $\mathcal{K}_{LBGU}$

4.3   LBGU-EM Algorithm

LBGU-EM algorithm consist of an initial run of LBG-U to find reference vectors $\{\mathbf{w}_c | c \in \mathcal{A}\}$ and their Voronoi sets $\{\mathcal{V}_c | c \in \mathcal{A}\}$. Thereafter the parameters of the mixture models are initialized. Let $\mathcal{V}_j$ be a Voronoi set of a center $\boldsymbol{\mu}_j$ and N be the number of all data points. Initial values of the model parameters for EM are set as follows:

1. Mixing parameters π_j is considered as a prior probabilities and initialized as fraction of data points in Voronoi regions j:

$$\pi_j = \frac{|\mathcal{V}_j|}{N}. \tag{4.3.1}$$

2. The means parameters $\boldsymbol{\mu}_j$ are initialized by means of data points in the Voronoi region j:

$$\boldsymbol{\mu}_j = \frac{1}{|\mathcal{V}_j|} \sum_{\boldsymbol{x} \in \mathcal{V}_j} \boldsymbol{x}. \tag{4.3.2}$$

3. The covariance parameters are initialized by covariances of Voronoi sets. Indeed, they depend on the type of covariance matrix. For example, for spherical covariance the initialization of the parameters can be given by

$$\sigma_j^2 = \frac{1}{d|\mathcal{V}_j|} \sum_{\boldsymbol{x} \in \mathcal{V}_j} \|\boldsymbol{x} - \boldsymbol{\mu}_j\|^2. \tag{4.3.3}$$

Thereafter, standard EM algorithm is run until convergence.

4.4   Experimental Results

A number of experiments were performed to compare the negative log-likelihood as the result of the LBGU-EM, LBG-EM, and random-EM algorithms using three datasets:

Data set A 2-dimensional noisy 11 components gaussian mixture

Data set B 3-dimensional noisy 4 components gaussian mixture

Data set C 34-dimensional dataset. This data set is the ionosphere dataset from UCI Machine Learning repository (Blake & Merz, 1998).

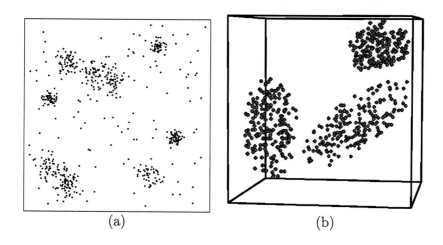

(a)   (b)

Figure 4.1: (a) Two-dimensional data, data set A. (b) Three-dimensional data, data set B.

For datasets A and B experiments were performed using 19 different codebook sizes (2, 3, ..., 20) and for dataset C with sizes (2, 3, 4 and 5). For each codebook size 20 trials were considered. For dataset C on trials up to size 5 were performed, because beyond this size the solutions being trapped to singularities for all methods.

The same initialization for the parameters σ_j^2 and $P(j)$ was used in each case. The initializations of σ_j^2 and $P(j)$ are employed to the Voronoi sets of their reference vectors as defined by LBGU-EM algorithm. Initialization for LBG and LBG-U was based on randomly sampling from the dataset $\mathcal{D}$.

In each experiment the negative log-likelihood and the number of EM iterations required until convergence were monitored. The both were used as performance measures of LBGU-EM, LBG-EM and random-EM algorithm. The experiment results are shown in Figure 4.2, 4.3 and 4.4.

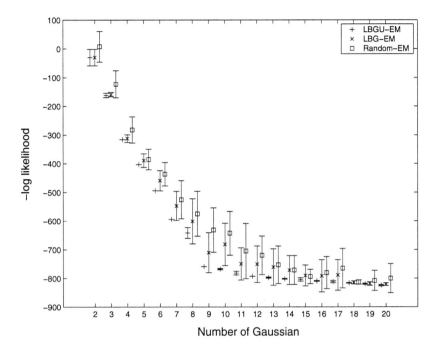

Figure 4.2: Mean of negative log-likelihood and variance values for dataset A.

As shown in Figure 4.2, 4.3 and 4.4, it is evident that for dataset A, B and C the mean of negative log-likelihood of the proposed LBGU-EM method is generally lower than the other two methods. And even, the result of the variance LBGU-EM is clearly smaller than those of the other initialization methods.

4.5   Conclusion

In this chapter how LBG-U algorithm can be used to improve the performance of the EM algorithm has been presented. Some experiments have

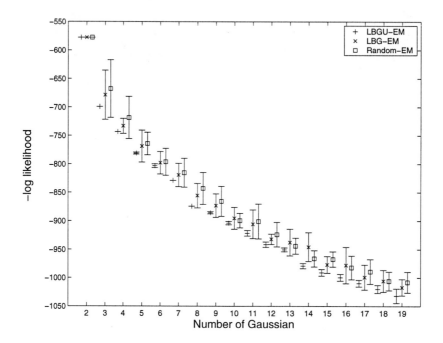

Figure 4.3:   Mean of negative log-likelihood and variance values for dataset B.

been performed to compare the performance of EM using three differ-ent techniques, random-, LBG- and LBGU- initialization. The results of the performed experiments showed superiority of LBGU-EM in improv-ing performance of EM compared with LBG and randomly initialized EM. The result of experiments using three datasets indicate that the use of LBG-U for EM initialization leads to lower variances of the resulting negative log-likelihood and thus to better reliability of the results. The achieved means of negative log-likelihoods using LBGU-EM were lower than those of both LBG and randomly initialized EM. On these data our experiments showed that LBGU-EM outperformed LBG-EM and EM with random initialization.

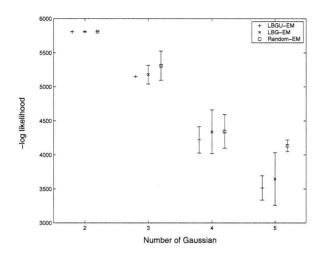

Figure 4.4: Mean of negative log-likelihood and variance values for dataset C.

A better characterization of the data sets, however, for which LBGU-EM gives an improvement is still an open problem. Since LBG-U minimizes a different objective function than density estimation, it may also be possible to create variance of LBG or LBG-U which take this into account.

CHAPTER 5
Classification Using Labeled and Unlabeled Data

In Chapter 3 we have discussed learning of mixture models for classification problems under supervised learning framework. In the problems, training data sets are labeled with class labels. The goal is to estimate the class-conditional densities to construct classifier systems.

In many applications, however, classifiers require a large number of labeled data to construct classifiers accurately. Unfortunately, much of the labeling task may require expensive human expertise for each training example, e.g. consider in domains such as medical image, geological image and remote sensing. In other domains such as speech- and character-recognition, text and web documents classification, the labeling may an arduous task and time-consuming. While obtaining large quantities of unlabeled data in almost all practical situation is very cheap and easy. In the domains such as stock exchange and internet search engines, even a large unlabeled data are free and directly available.

Given labeled and unlabeled data, traditional approaches will fall between two choice, either supervised or unsupervised learning. When supervised learning technique is applied, it cannot take advantage from the unlabeled data. On the other hand, unsupervised learning can model distribution of the data, but it can not exploit their labels. In order to take the advantage both of labeled and unlabeled data, recently there have been a number of attempts inspired *semi-supervised* learning methods by combining supervised and unsupervised learning for constructing classifiers. The motivation is that the classification error of classifiers build by augmenting unlabeled data into labeled training data sets may be lower than the error obtained when the classifiers are build on the basis of the labeled data alone. An extensive review on this theme appears in (Seeger, 2001). A number of existing algorithms to improve learning by using unlabeled data also were presented in several workshops such as NIPS-1998, NIPS-1999 and NIPS-2000.

From the literature we noted some important points that can be further analysis. First, theoretical and empirical studies showed that unlabeled data can *improve*, but can also *degrade* performance of classification. Most authors emphasized that the structure of the generative model plays important role on this phenomenon (Castelli & Cover, 1996; Shahshahani & Landgrebe, 1994; Baluja, 1998; Nigam *et al.*, 2000; Cozman & Cohen, 2001). Some authors (Baluja, 1998; Nigam *et al.*, 2000) guessed that the use of unlabeled data require a closer *match* between the data and the generative model. In (Cozman & Cohen, 2001; Cozman *et al.*, 2003) authors attempted to derive a detailed analysis of the performance degradation and concluded that unlabeled data can degrade performance when the classifier assumes an *incorrect* structure. However, they were also aware that it is possible additional sources of performance degradation can be found (Cozman & Cohen, 2001). Second, the regularization method (Nigam *et al.*, 2000) was proposed to adjust strength of unlabeled data contribution. The method is to obtain an optimal classifier given additional unlabeled data, when a correct structure of the generative model can not be found. However, the method is still debatable as criticized in (Cozman *et al.*, 2003), in which they did not observe improvement of classification by varying weighting factors as claimed by Nigam et al.

Although there have been many studies on the labeled and unlabeled data problem, the existing efforts, however, do not investigate the *overfitting* condition. Therefore, this chapter addresses to clarify the relation of model complexity and effect of additional unlabeled data, especially when classifiers have very complex structure and *overfitting* condition. We shall also propose a novel regularization method using the *regularized* weighting factors. The method is to adjust the strength of labeled/unlabeled data's contribution. Our method is different with the method in (Nigam *et al.*, 2000) in the form of the weighting factors. We conducted empirical studies by taking generalization error into account.

The rest of this Chapter is organized as follows. In the section 5.1 we give review on the previous research on labeled and unlabeled data problem. Thereafter, a brief background describing the semi-supervised learning for gaussian mixture model is provided in section 5.2. In section 5.2.2 the algorithms for learning of gaussian mixture models are described, especially for complex models which allow us to represent class-conditional densities using multiple components of mixture. Section 5.3 is devoted to introduce our regularization method to adjust the strength of contribution of labeled/unlabeled data. The experimental results are presented in section 5.4 and the conclusion is given in the last section.

5.1   Related Work

The earlier works on this theme including (O'Neill, 1978; Ganesalingam & McLachlan, 1978; Ganesalingam & McLachlan, 1979; Titterington *et al.*, 1985) gave positive motivation to take advantage of the unlabeled data for classification tasks. By concerning on mixtures of two gaussians with equal covariances and well-separated they notified that the asymptotical gain of using unlabeled data is significant. Unfortunately, the conditioned assumptions seem to be unrealistic, whereas the classes may not well-separated and the quadratic boundaries are produced when the classes are gaussian with different covariance matrices. In many situations even it is necessary to construct classifiers with more complex models to create complex boundaries.

In recent years, several authors investigated the same theme both theoretically and experimentally (Castelli & Cover, 1996; Ratsaby & Venkatesh, 1995; Shahshahani & Landgrebe, 1994; Baluja, 1998; Nigam *et al.*, 2000; Zhang & Oles, 2000; Cozman *et al.*, 2003). The investigation was aimed toward the general question whether additional unlabeled data can help in enhancing the classification performance. Some particularly interesting results will be presented in the following paragraph.

Shahshahani and Landgrebe (Shahshahani & Landgrebe, 1994) studied the effect of additional unlabeled data in enhancing the classification performance. They performed experiments using gaussian mixture models-based classifiers for remote sensing image understanding. They reported that unlabeled data can help to *increase* classification performance under assuming that the classifiers are unbiased. They observed also that the use of additional unlabeled data may *decreases* classification accuracy. However, there are some loopholes in their arguments. They did not define generative models clearly and did not investigate the generalization error. Arguments of Shahshahani and Landgrebe are also

vague in explanation of degradation phenomena. They speculated that
the degradation may be due to by outliers or by data of unknown classes.
Their arguments also are somewhat unclear dan confuse in the explaining
of the phenomena, as also criticized in other papers (Zhang & Oles, 2000;
Seeger, 2001; Cozman & Cohen, 2001).

Theoretical studies aimed at understanding the value of unlabeled
data have been conducted by Castelli and Cover (Castelli & Cover, 1996)
and Ratsaby and Vankatesh (Ratsaby & Venkatesh, 1995). They investigated the tradeoff between labeled and unlabeled data complexity in
learning classifiers based gaussian mixture models for a two-class problem.
Under assumption that the density of the unlabeled data is identifiable
and training sets are composed of an infinite number of unlabeled data
they reported that unlabeled data can help in reducing the probability
of error. Specifically, Castelli and Cover (Castelli & Cover, 1996) studied
the value of unlabeled data under assumptions above they proved that
classification error decreases exponentially with the number of labeled
data and linearly with the number of unlabeled data. These studies en-
force the results of empirical study of (Shahshahani & Landgrebe, 1994)
about enhancing classification performance using unlabeled data. However, they do not investigate model complexity and degradation phenomena as reported in (Shahshahani & Landgrebe, 1994), so that some basic
questions remain unclear.

The similar result was informed by Baluja (Baluja, 1998) in his study
on a face orientation classification problem using Naive Bayes classifiers.
From some experimental results he observed significant performance improvement by using unlabeled data over using labeled data alone. However, unlabeled data may *hurt* performance of classification when a large
amount of labeled data were presented for training. He argued that the
degradation may be caused by un-matching generative models to the un-

derlying distribution.

An intensive study on this theme was conducted by Nigam et al. (Nigam *et al.*, 2000) for a text classification task using Naive Bayes classifiers. They reported similar results as reported by Baluja (Baluja, 1998), that unlabeled data can either improve or degrade performance of the classifiers. They emphasize that the use of unlabeled data require a closer *match* between the data and the generative models. Furthermore, they proposed a method of regularization so that an optimal classifiers can be obtained. They showed that by adjusting a weighting factor, significant improvement of classification can be achieved. However, the proposed method is still debatable as criticized in (Cozman *et al.*, 2003). In the work of Cozman et al. they found that by varying the values of the weighting factor the unlabeled data can not improve performance of classification as claimed by Nigam et al.

The study of Cozman et al. in (Cozman & Cohen, 2001; Cozman *et al.*, 2003) focus on degradation phenomena when unlabeled data added to the training data set. They concluded that unlabeled data can *degrade* classification performance if the classifier assumes an *incorrect* structure. They defined the correct structure as structure of underlying distribution generated the data and incorrect structure to any other structure. They have derived a detailed analysis of this phenomena in terms of asymptotic bias. However, they were also aware that it is possible that additional sources of performance degradation can be found.

5.2   Semi-Supervised Learning

In the previous chapter we have presented the supervised learning, in which classifiers are given a set of labeled data only. In this chapter we consider another learning paradigm so-called *semi-supervised learning* which uses not only labeled data but also unlabeled data for training the classifiers. Such learning problem is known also as labeled and unlabeled data problem (Seeger, 2001). Usually, the size of unlabeled data set is much larger than labeled data set.

Clearly, this is an incomplete data problem since only a part of the training data is labeled and most of the data are unlabeled. Furthermore, this problem will be handled using EM algorithm (Dempster *et al.*, 1977) by considering a missing-data mechanism as introduced by Little and Rubin (Little & Rubin, 1987). This mechanism allows us to regard the class labels of data set as missing values that should be estimated.

5.2.1 Learning of Simple Models

We consider now the data set that consist of c classes, each data point is assigned to one of c class labels $\mathcal{C} = \{C_1, ..., C_c\}$. Let $\mathcal{D}_l$ be the set of labeled data of N_l data points and $\mathcal{D}_u$ be the set of unlabeled data of N_u data points, then the training data set is given by $\mathcal{D} = \mathcal{D}_l \cup \mathcal{D}_u$. The labeled data set consist of pairs $(\boldsymbol{x}_i, \boldsymbol{z}_i)$ of input vectors $\boldsymbol{x}_i$ and class-label $\boldsymbol{z}_i$ as follows

$$\mathcal{D}_l = \{(\boldsymbol{x}_1, \boldsymbol{z}_1), ..., (\boldsymbol{x}_{N_l}, \boldsymbol{z}_{N_l})\},$$

while the unlabeled data set consist of only input vectors (without class labels)

$$\mathcal{D}_u = \{\boldsymbol{x}_{N_l+1}, ..., \boldsymbol{x}_N\},$$

where N is the size of training data set. The variable $\boldsymbol{z}_i \in \mathcal{C}$ indicates class label of input vector $\boldsymbol{x}_i$ with elements are defined by

$$z_{ki} = \begin{cases} 1, & \text{if } \boldsymbol{x}_i \text{ belong to class } C_k; \\ 0, & \text{others.} \end{cases} \tag{5.2.1}$$

First, we consider a simple problem in which each class of the data set is regarded to be generated from one component density of mixture. Since there are one-to-one correspondence between the components and the classes, class labels are identic with component labels, so that the number

of classes is same as the number of mixture components. For this purpose
we can construct a gaussian mixture model of M component densities to
model c class-probability densities, $p(\boldsymbol{x}|C_1), ..., p(\boldsymbol{x}|C_c)$. Mixture models
therefore are given in the form

$$p(x|\boldsymbol{\Psi}) = \sum_{k=1}^{M} \pi_j p(\boldsymbol{x}|\boldsymbol{\theta}_j), \qquad (5.2.2)$$

where $\boldsymbol{\Psi}$ is a vector of the mixture parameters. Here, π_j is the mixing
coefficient and $p(\boldsymbol{x}|\boldsymbol{\theta}_k)$ is the conditional probability density. In this case
a conditional probability density $p(\boldsymbol{x}|\boldsymbol{\theta}_k)$ represents a class-conditional
density $p(\boldsymbol{x}|C_k)$ and the mixing parameter π_k represents the prior pro-
bability of class C_j.

Since the training data set consist of labeled and unlabeled data set
and by assuming that the data set were drawn i.i.d. from an underlying
distribution, the log-likelihood can be written in the form (McLachlan &
Peel, 2000)

$$\mathcal{L}(\mathcal{D}|\boldsymbol{\Psi}) = \mathcal{L}_l(\mathcal{D}_l|\boldsymbol{\Psi}) + \mathcal{L}_u(\mathcal{D}_u|\boldsymbol{\Psi}), \qquad (5.2.3)$$

where $\mathcal{L}_l$ and $\mathcal{L}_u$ are the log-likelihood of labeled and unlabeled data
respectively. Using notation of class labels as in (5.2.1) the log-likelihood
can be completely written in the form

$$\begin{aligned}\mathcal{L}(\mathcal{D}|\boldsymbol{\Psi}) &= \sum_{\boldsymbol{x}_i \in \mathcal{D}_\ell} \sum_j z_{ji} \ln \pi_j p(\boldsymbol{x}_i|\theta_j) \\ &+ \sum_{\boldsymbol{x}_i \in \mathcal{D}_u} \ln \sum_j \pi_j p(\boldsymbol{x}_i|\theta_j). \qquad (5.2.4)\end{aligned}$$

The first term of (5.2.4) represents the complete-data log-likelihood, since
all data points in $\mathcal{D}_l$ are labeled, while the second term of (5.2.4) represents incomplete-data log-likelihood. The incompleteness is caused by
unavailability of the component labels of unlabeled data in $\mathcal{D}_u$. Learning
algorithm then is turned for maximizing the log-likelihood.

For unlabeled data, we introduce a *hypothetical* complete data set $\mathcal{D}^c$, in which each data point is labeled with hypothetical component which generated it. Our complete data set can be written in the form

$$\begin{aligned} \mathcal{D}^c \quad = \quad & \{(\boldsymbol{x}_1, \boldsymbol{z}_1), ..., (\boldsymbol{x}_{N_l}, \boldsymbol{z}_{N_l}), \\ & (\boldsymbol{x}_{N_l+1}, \boldsymbol{y}_{N_l+1}), ..., (\boldsymbol{x}_N, \boldsymbol{y}_N)\}, \end{aligned}$$

where $\boldsymbol{z}_i$ are class labels of labeled data and $\boldsymbol{y}_i \equiv (y_{i1}, ..., y_{iM})^T$ is a hypothetical class label with elements $y_{ji} \in \{1, 0\}$ representing whether a data point $\boldsymbol{x}_i \in \mathcal{D}_u$ is regarded or not regarded to be generated from component j of the mixture. The hypothetical complete-data log-likelihood therefore can be written in the form

$$\begin{aligned} \mathcal{L}^c(\mathcal{D}^c|\Psi) \quad = \quad & \sum_{\boldsymbol{x}_i \in \mathcal{D}_\ell} \sum_{j=1}^{c} z_{ji} \ln \pi_j p(\boldsymbol{x}_i|\theta_j) \\ & + \sum_{\boldsymbol{x}_i \in \mathcal{D}_u} \sum_{j=1}^{c} y_{ji} \ln \pi_j p(\boldsymbol{x}_i|\theta_j). \end{aligned} \qquad (5.2.5)$$

In order to maximize the log-likelihood (5.2.5) we can employ EM algorithm, an iterative algorithm that consists of two steps, expectation step (E-step) and maximization step (M-Step). Using EM, the likelihood is increased in every step and a local maximum can be achieved.

E-Step

In E-step we compute the expectation of the complete-data log-likelihood $\mathcal{Q}(\Psi; \Psi^{(t)})$ as follows

$$\mathcal{Q}(\Psi; \Psi^{(t)}) = \mathcal{E}_{\Psi^{(t)}}[\mathcal{L}^c(\mathcal{D}^c|\Psi)]. \qquad (5.2.6)$$

Since the complete-data log-likelihood (5.2.5) is a linear function of class labels, then the expected complete-data log-likelihood depends only on the expectation values $\mathcal{E}[y_{ji}]$ that are given by posterior probabilities of component memberships as follows

$$P(j|\boldsymbol{x}_i) = \frac{\pi_j p_j(\boldsymbol{x}_i|\boldsymbol{\theta}_j)}{\sum_{j=1}^c \pi_j p_j(\boldsymbol{x}_i|\boldsymbol{\theta}_j)}, \tag{5.2.7}$$

see (McLachlan & Peel, 2000) for more detail. The expectation of complete-data log-likelihood therefore is given by

$$\begin{aligned} \mathcal{Q}(\boldsymbol{\Psi};\boldsymbol{\Psi}^t) &= \sum_{\boldsymbol{x}_i \in \mathcal{D}_\ell} \sum_{j=1}^c z_{ji} \ln \pi_j p(\boldsymbol{x}_i|\boldsymbol{\theta}_j) \\ &+ \sum_{\boldsymbol{x}_i \in \mathcal{D}_u} \sum_{j=1}^c P(j|\boldsymbol{x}_i) \ln \pi_j p(\boldsymbol{x}_i|\boldsymbol{\theta}_j). \end{aligned} \tag{5.2.8}$$

M-Step

In M-step we estimate parameters of the mixture $\boldsymbol{\Psi}^{(t+1)}$ that maximize the expectation of complete-data log-likelihood (5.2.8). The necessary equations to update parameters of mixture for every step of EM can be found by differentiating (5.2.8) respect to the parameters, then setting the derivatives to zero

$$\nabla_{\psi_j} \mathcal{Q}(\boldsymbol{\Psi};\boldsymbol{\Psi}^{(t)}) = 0, \tag{5.2.9}$$

where ψ_j is the corresponding parameters of components of mixture.

For gaussian mixture models the component densities are parameterized by mean vectors and covariance matrices $\{\boldsymbol{\mu}_j, \boldsymbol{\Sigma}_j\}$. The update equations needed to maximize the expectation of complete-data log-likelihood (5.2.8) for means, mixing and covariance parameters are as follows

$$\boldsymbol{\mu}_j^{(t+1)} = \frac{\sum_{\boldsymbol{x}_i \in \mathcal{D}} P(j|\boldsymbol{x}_i)^{(t)} \boldsymbol{x}_i}{\sum_{\boldsymbol{x}_i \in \mathcal{D}} P(j|\boldsymbol{x}_i)^{(t)}} \tag{5.2.10}$$

$$\pi_j^{(t+1)} = \frac{1}{N} \sum_{\boldsymbol{x}_i \in \mathcal{D}} P(j|\boldsymbol{x}_i)^{(t)} \tag{5.2.11}$$

$$\boldsymbol{\Sigma}_j^{(t+1)} = \frac{\sum_{\boldsymbol{x}_i \in \mathcal{D}} P(j|\boldsymbol{x}_i)^{(t)} (\boldsymbol{x}_i - \boldsymbol{\mu}_j^{(t+1)})(\boldsymbol{x}_i - \boldsymbol{\mu}_j^{(t+1)})^T}{\sum_{\boldsymbol{x}_i \in \mathcal{D}} P(j|\boldsymbol{x}_i)^{(t)}}, \tag{5.2.12}$$

where the posterior probabilities of component memberships $P(j|\boldsymbol{x})$ are given in the form

$$P(j|\boldsymbol{x}_i)^{(t+1)} = \begin{cases} z_{ji}, & \boldsymbol{x}_i \in \mathcal{D}_\ell \\ \dfrac{\pi_j^{(t)} p_j(\boldsymbol{x}_i|\boldsymbol{\theta}_j^{(t)})}{\sum_{j=1}^c \pi_j^{(t)} p_j(\boldsymbol{x}_i|\boldsymbol{\theta}_j^{(t)})}, & \boldsymbol{x}_i \in \mathcal{D}_u \end{cases} \qquad (5.2.13)$$

The complete semi-supervised learning algorithm of gaussian mixture models with single component per class is presented in Algorithm 6.

Algorithm 6 Semi-supervised learning of GMM

---

1. **Input:** Training data set $\mathcal{D} = \mathcal{D}_\ell \cup \mathcal{D}_u$.

2. **Initialize:**
   - parameters of mixture model $\boldsymbol{\Psi}^0$, e.g. by using $k-$Means.
   - compute the posterior probabilities $P^{(0)}(j|\mathbf{x})$ using $\boldsymbol{\Psi}^0$.

3. **Do for** $t = 0, ..., t_m$

   (a) E-Step: evaluate expected values (5.2.8) by computing the component memberships given the current parameters $\boldsymbol{\Psi}^{(t)}$ using (5.2.13).

   (b) M-Step: maximize (5.2.8) by estimating $\boldsymbol{\Psi}^{(t+1)}$ given $P^{(t+1)}(j|\mathbf{x}_i)$ using upgrade equations in Eq. (2.3.8) for mean, (2.3.9) for mixing and (2.3.10) for covariance parameters.

4. **Break if** $|\Delta \mathcal{L}| \leq \epsilon$, ϵ is a small arbitrary number.

5. **Output:** Parameter estimate $\boldsymbol{\Psi}$.

5.2.2   Learning of Complex Models

In practice usually more complex models are necessary to construct classifiers what with complex data sets, in which the group structure of the data can not be modelled entirely using simple models. Model complexity plays important role in developing generative models especially in the reducing of bias of expected error. By structure we mean the set of constraints that must be satisfied by parameters of the classifiers. Complex models allow us to create quadratic or more complex boundaries, so that optimal classifiers can be attained. Obviously, the classifiers built using more complex models are more powerful in terms of its ability to discriminate among various class of different shapes. Indeed, the complexity of the model should be taken in accordance with the given training data into account.

In this section we consider complex models governed by the number of component densities to model the class-conditional densities. For a given fixed structure, estimating the model's parameters can be done using a maximum-likelihood approach. To handle this problem the learning algorithm can be derived from learning algorithm based on EM as in Section 3.5.2. Here, however, there are new missing values and an additional constrain. Although a part of training examples is labeled, however, which component of the mixture generated them is unknown. This problem then can be regarded as incomplete data problem and can be be tackled using EM.

Here, we shall investigate only two classes classification problems. Suppose the mixture models are built using M component densities

$$p(\boldsymbol{x}|\boldsymbol{\Psi}) = \sum_{j=1}^{M} \pi_j p(\boldsymbol{x}|\boldsymbol{\theta}_j), \qquad (5.2.14)$$

where $M > 2$. We assume that a set of mixture components generating data points of each class are known. We can therefore label every mixture component j with a class label vector $\boldsymbol{t}_j$ according to which class it belongs to, $(j, \boldsymbol{t}_j), j = 1, ..., M$. The class label of mixture component can be represented as a vector $\boldsymbol{t}_j = (t_{j1}, ..., t_{jc})^T$ with elements $t_{kj} \in \{1, 0\}$ are defined as follows

$$t_{kj} = \begin{cases} 1, & \text{if component } j \text{ belongs to class } C_k; \\ 0, & \text{others.} \end{cases} \qquad (5.2.15)$$

Since the component labels for every data points unavailable, we consider a hypothetical complete data set, in which each data point is labeled with a label of component which generated it. We introduce a set class labels $\{y_i | i = 1, ..., N\}$ corresponding to the data points $x_i \in \mathcal{D}$, where $y_i = (y_{i1}, ..., y_{iM})^T$ with elements $y_{ji} \in \{1, 0\}$ represents whether a data point x_i is regarded or not regarded generated from component j of the mixture. Using hypothetical component labels of each data points, the complete-data log-likelihood therefore can be written in the form

$$
\begin{aligned}
\mathcal{L}^c(\boldsymbol{\Psi}; \mathcal{D}^c) \;=\; & \sum_{x_i \in \mathcal{D}_\ell} \sum_j y_{ji} \ln \pi_j p(x_i | \boldsymbol{\theta}_j) \\
& + \sum_{x_i \in \mathcal{D}_u} \sum_j y_{ji} \ln \pi_j p(x_i | \boldsymbol{\theta}_j),
\end{aligned}
\tag{5.2.16}
$$

where $\mathcal{D}^c = \{(x_i, y_i) | x_i \in \mathcal{D}_\ell \cup \mathcal{D}_u\}$ is the hypothetical complete data set.

Again, we consider a learning algorithm based on EM for estimating the maximum-likelihood under new constrains above.

E-Step

In the E-step we compute expectation values of the complete-data log-likelihood (5.2.16)

$$
\mathcal{Q}(\boldsymbol{\Psi}; \boldsymbol{\Psi}^{(t)}) = \mathcal{E}_{\boldsymbol{\Psi}^{(t)}}[\mathcal{L}^c(\boldsymbol{\Psi}; \mathcal{D}^c)],
\tag{5.2.17}
$$

where $\boldsymbol{\Psi}^{(t)}$ is the parameter estimates from previous iteration. Obviously, the expectation value depends only on the expectation of component memberships $\mathcal{E}[y_{ji}]$ that are given by the posterior probabilities of component memberships

$$
P(j | x_i) = \frac{\pi_j p(x_i | j)}{\sum_j \pi_j p(x_i | j)}
\tag{5.2.18}
$$

In our case, due to the constrain that the components of mixture were partitioned into some different classes, the posterior probabilities $P(j | x_i)$

may not be used directly for computing the expectation of complete-data log-likelihood (5.2.17). We must restrict therefore the component memberships for the labeled examples $x \in \mathcal{D}_\ell$, since the examples have been generated from certain class. Indeed, data points x_i of class $\mathcal{C}_k$ have to be generated only by components of mixture from the same class, $t_j \in \mathcal{C}_k$. In other word the constrain $z_i = t_j$ must be satisfied. Therefore we introduce the *restricted* component membership $\tau(j|x)$ in the form

$$\tau(j|x_i) = \frac{\delta_{t_j,z_i} P(j|x_i)}{\sum_{j=1}^{M} \delta_{t_j,z_i} P(j|x_i)}, \qquad (5.2.19)$$

where

$$\delta_{t_j,z_i} = \begin{cases} 1, & \text{if } t_j = z_i; \\ 0, & \text{if } t_j \neq z_i. \end{cases} \qquad (5.2.20)$$

The denominator of (5.2.19) is to ensure that the sum is unity

$$\sum_j \tau(j|x) = 1.$$

The expectation of complete-data log-likelihood therefore is written in the form

$$\begin{aligned} \mathcal{Q}(\Psi; \Psi^t) &= \sum_{x_i \in \mathcal{D}_\ell} \sum_j \tau^{(t)}(j|x_i) \ln \pi_j p(x_i|\theta_j) \\ &+ \sum_{x_i \in \mathcal{D}_u} \sum_j P(j|x_i)^{(t)} \ln \pi_j p(x_i|\theta_j) \qquad (5.2.21) \end{aligned}$$

Since the values of $\pi_j^{(t)}$ and $\theta_j^{(t)}$ to compute $\tau^{(t)}(j|x_i)$ are fixed, the expectation $\mathcal{Q}(\Psi; \Psi^t)$ is a function of the parameters π_j and θ_j. Hence, in expectation-step of EM we should compute the component memberships $P(j|x_i)^{(t)}$ and $\tau(j|x_i)^{(t)}$ using previous computed parameters Ψ^t.

M-Step

In maximization-step of EM the parameters of mixture $\Psi^{(t+1)}$ are estimated by maximizing the expectation of complete-data log-likelihood.

Update equations to maximizing the expectation for every step can be obtained by differentiating the expected complete-data log-likelihood (5.2.21) respect to the parameters and set the derivatives to zero

$$\nabla_{\psi_j} \mathcal{Q}(\boldsymbol{\Psi}; \boldsymbol{\Psi}^{(t)}) = 0. \tag{5.2.22}$$

For gaussian mixture models with means and covariance parameters are $\boldsymbol{\mu}_j$ and $\boldsymbol{\Sigma}_j$ respectively, the update equations for M-step can be found in the form

$$\widehat{\pi}_j = \frac{\sum_{\boldsymbol{x}_i^l} \tau(j|\boldsymbol{x}_i^l) + \sum_{\boldsymbol{x}_i^u} P(j|\boldsymbol{x}_i^u)}{N_l + N_u} \tag{5.2.23}$$

$$\widehat{\boldsymbol{\mu}}_j = \frac{\sum_{\boldsymbol{x}_i^l} \tau(j|\boldsymbol{x}_i^l)\boldsymbol{x}_i^l + \sum_{\boldsymbol{x}_i^u} P(j|\boldsymbol{x}_i^u)\boldsymbol{x}_i^u}{\sum_{\boldsymbol{x}_i^l} \tau(j|\boldsymbol{x}_i^l) + \sum_{\boldsymbol{x}_i^u} P(j|\boldsymbol{x}_i^u)} \tag{5.2.24}$$

$$\widehat{\boldsymbol{\Sigma}}_j = \frac{\sum_{\boldsymbol{x}_i^l} \tau(j|\boldsymbol{x}_i^l)(\boldsymbol{x}_i^l - \widehat{\boldsymbol{\mu}}_j)(\boldsymbol{x}_i^l - \widehat{\boldsymbol{\mu}}_j)^T + \sum_{\boldsymbol{x}_i^u} P(j|\boldsymbol{x}_i^u)(\boldsymbol{x}_i^u - \widehat{\boldsymbol{\mu}}_j)(\boldsymbol{x}_i^u - \widehat{\boldsymbol{\mu}}_j)^T}{\sum_{\boldsymbol{x}_i^l} \tau(j|\boldsymbol{x}_i^l) + \sum_{\boldsymbol{x}_i^u} P(j|\boldsymbol{x}_i^u)}, \tag{5.2.25}$$

where $\boldsymbol{x}_i^l \equiv \boldsymbol{x}_i \in \mathcal{D}_\ell$ and $\boldsymbol{x}_i^u \equiv \boldsymbol{x}_i \in \mathcal{D}_u$. The complete semi-supervised learning algorithm of complex models with multiple components per class can be found in Algorithm 7.

5.3   EM with Regularized Weighting Factor

In this section we will describe a novel algorithm, namely the extended-EM with regularized weighting factors. The algorithm introduces a new parameter so-called *regularized weighting factors* added to modulate the degree to which EM weights the labeled and unlabeled term of the log-likelihood (5.2.3). This algorithm is extended from (Nigam *et al.*, 2000), in which they proposed extended EM by weighting each term of the likelihood by a weighting factor $\mathcal{L}(\mathcal{D}|\boldsymbol{\Psi}) = \lambda_l \mathcal{L}_l(\mathcal{D}_l|\boldsymbol{\Psi}) + \lambda_u \mathcal{L}_u(\mathcal{D}_u|\boldsymbol{\Psi})$.

Algorithm 7 Semi-supervised learning of complex models

---

1. **Input:** Training data set $\mathcal{D}$ consisting of labeled data set $\mathcal{D}_l$ and unlabeled data set $\mathcal{D}_u$, $\mathcal{D} = \mathcal{D}_\ell \cup \mathcal{D}_u$. Labeled mixture components $\{(j, \mathbf{t}_j) | j = 1, .., M\}$.

2. **Initialize:** Model parameters $\boldsymbol{\Psi}^0$, component memberships $P^{(0)}(j|\mathbf{x})$ computed using $\boldsymbol{\Psi}^0$.

3. **Do for** $t = 0, ..., t_m$

   (a) E-Step: Evaluate the expectation of log-likelihood $\mathcal{Q}(\boldsymbol{\Psi}; \boldsymbol{\Psi}^{(t)})$ using Eq. (5.2.21) by computing the component memberships $P(j|\mathbf{x}_i)^{(t+1)}$ using current parameters $\boldsymbol{\Psi}^{(t)}$.

   (b) For all labeled data points $\mathbf{x}_i \in \mathcal{D}_l$: compute the restricted component memberships $\tau(j|\mathbf{x}_i)^{(t+1)}$ using Eq. (5.2.19) with $P(j|\mathbf{x}_i)^{(t+1)}$ as computed in (3a) above.

   (c) M-Step: Maximize the expectation $\mathcal{Q}(\boldsymbol{\Psi}; \boldsymbol{\Psi}^{(t)})$ by estimating model parameters $\boldsymbol{\Psi}^{(t+1)}$ given $P(j|\mathbf{x}_i)^{(t+1)}$ and $\tau(j|\mathbf{x}_i)^{(t+1)}$ using upgrade equations (5.2.23) for mixing, (5.2.24) for means and (5.2.25) covariance parameters.

4. **Break if** $|\Delta\mathcal{L}| \leq \epsilon$, ϵ is an arbitrary small number.

5. **Output:** Parameter estimate $\boldsymbol{\Psi}$.

Clearly, for a given certain value of λ_l the contribution of unlabeled data will be higher in line with the augmentation of unlabeled data.

Here, we propose a novel regularization method, in which the contribution's strength of the unlabeled data is not determined by the size of the data set but more by weighting factor itself. The contribution of unlabeled data can be fixed at a certain level and does not depend on the size of augmented unlabeled data. Our extended EM maximizes the following modified log-likelihood

$$\mathcal{L}(\boldsymbol{\Psi}; \mathcal{D}) = \left(\frac{\lambda_l}{N_l}\right) \mathcal{L}_l(\boldsymbol{\Psi}; \mathcal{D}_\ell) + \left(\frac{\lambda_u}{N_u}\right) \mathcal{L}_u(\boldsymbol{\Psi}; \mathcal{D}_u). \qquad (5.3.1)$$

The weighting factors λ_l and λ_u are any positive value

$$\lambda_l, \lambda_u \geq 0 \qquad (5.3.2)$$

representing strength of the labeled and unlabeled data contribution. Here, it is assumed also that

$$N_l, N_u > 0. \tag{5.3.3}$$

When $N_l = 0$ or $N_u = 0$ we should refers to the unsupervised learning as discussed in Chapter 2 or the supervised learning as in Chapter 3 respectively.

For the simplest model as in subsection 5.2.1 with single component per class, the modified log-likelihood is given by

$$
\begin{aligned}
\mathcal{L}(\mathcal{D}|\boldsymbol{\Psi}) = {} & \frac{\lambda_l}{N_l} \sum_{\boldsymbol{x}_i \in \mathcal{D}_\ell} \sum_j z_{ji} \ln \pi_j p(\boldsymbol{x}_i|\boldsymbol{\theta}_j) \\
& + \frac{\lambda_u}{N_u} \sum_{\boldsymbol{x}_i \in \mathcal{D}_u} \ln \sum_j \pi_j p(\boldsymbol{x}_i|\boldsymbol{\theta}_j).
\end{aligned}
\tag{5.3.4}
$$

In M-step, EM algorithm therefore maximizes the expected complete-data log-likelihood

$$
\begin{aligned}
\mathcal{Q}(\boldsymbol{\Psi}; \boldsymbol{\Psi}^{(t)}) = {} & \frac{\lambda_l}{N_l} \sum_{\boldsymbol{x}_i \in \mathcal{D}_\ell} \sum_j z_{ji} \ln \pi_j p(\boldsymbol{x}_i|\boldsymbol{\theta}_j) \\
& + \frac{\lambda_u}{N_u} \sum_{\boldsymbol{x}_i \in \mathcal{D}_u} \sum_j P(j|\boldsymbol{x}_i) \ln \pi_j p(\boldsymbol{x}_i|\boldsymbol{\theta}_j)
\end{aligned}
\tag{5.3.5}
$$

respect to the mixture parameters $\boldsymbol{\Psi}$. By setting derivatives of (5.3.5) to zero, $\nabla_{\boldsymbol{\Psi}} \mathcal{Q}(\boldsymbol{\Psi}; \boldsymbol{\Psi}^{(t)}) = 0$, the update equations can be found as follows

$$
\widehat{\pi}_j = \frac{1}{\lambda_l + \lambda_u} \left(\frac{\lambda_l}{N_l} \sum_{\boldsymbol{x}_i^l} z_{ji} + \frac{\lambda_u}{N_u} \sum_{\boldsymbol{x}_i^u} P(j|\boldsymbol{x}_i^u) \right)
\tag{5.3.6}
$$

$$
\widehat{\boldsymbol{\mu}}_j = \frac{\frac{\lambda_l}{N_l} \sum_{\boldsymbol{x}_i^l} z_{ji} \boldsymbol{x}_i^l + \frac{\lambda_u}{N_u} \sum_{\boldsymbol{x}_i^u} P(j|\boldsymbol{x}_i^u) \boldsymbol{x}_i^u}{\frac{\lambda_l}{N_l} \sum_{\boldsymbol{x}_i^l} z_{ji} + \frac{\lambda_u}{N_u} \sum_{\boldsymbol{x}_i^u} P(j|\boldsymbol{x}_i^u)}
\tag{5.3.7}
$$

$$
\widehat{\boldsymbol{\Sigma}}_j = \frac{\frac{\lambda_l}{N_l} \sum_{\boldsymbol{x}_i^l} z_{ji} (\boldsymbol{x}_i^l - \widehat{\boldsymbol{\mu}}_j)(\boldsymbol{x}_i^l - \widehat{\boldsymbol{\mu}}_j)^T + \frac{\lambda_u}{N_u} \sum_{\boldsymbol{x}_i^u} P(j|\boldsymbol{x}_i^u)(\boldsymbol{x}_i^u - \widehat{\boldsymbol{\mu}}_j)(\boldsymbol{x}_i^u - \widehat{\boldsymbol{\mu}}_j)^T}{\frac{\lambda_l}{N_l} \sum_{\boldsymbol{x}_i^l} z_{ji} + \frac{\lambda_u}{N_u} \sum_{\boldsymbol{x}_i^u} P(j|\boldsymbol{x}_i^u)},
\tag{5.3.8}
$$

where $\boldsymbol{x}_i^l \in \boldsymbol{x}_i \in \mathcal{D}_\ell$ and $\boldsymbol{x}_i^u \in \boldsymbol{x}_i \in \mathcal{D}_u$.

Similarly, for complex models with multiple component per class as discussed in section 5.2.2, the log-likelihood is modified by parameterizing both terms of $\mathcal{L}_l$ and $\mathcal{L}_u$ with $\frac{\lambda_l}{N_l}$ and $\frac{\lambda_u}{N_u}$ respectively. In M-step of EM therefore we maximize the following expectation of complete log-likelihood

$$
\mathcal{Q}(\boldsymbol{\Psi}; \boldsymbol{\Psi}^{(t)}) \;=\; \frac{\lambda_l}{N_l} \sum_{\boldsymbol{x}_i \in \mathcal{D}_\ell} \sum_{j=1}^{M} \tau^{(t)}(j|\boldsymbol{x}_i) \ln \pi_j p(\boldsymbol{x}_i|\boldsymbol{\theta}_j)
$$

$$
+\; \frac{\lambda_u}{N_u} \sum_{\boldsymbol{x}_i \in \mathcal{D}_u} \sum_{j=1}^{M} P^{(t)}(j|\boldsymbol{x}_i) \ln \pi_j p(\boldsymbol{x}_i|\boldsymbol{\theta}_j), \quad (5.3.9)
$$

where $P(j|\boldsymbol{x}_i)^{(t)}$ and $\tau(j|\boldsymbol{x}_i)^{(t)}$ are computed using (5.2.18) and (5.2.19). For gaussian mixtures, therefore, the update equations are of the form

$$
\widehat{\pi}_j \;=\; \frac{1}{\lambda_l + \lambda_u} \left(\frac{\lambda_l}{N_l} \sum_{\boldsymbol{x}_i^l} \tau(j|\boldsymbol{x}_i^l) + \frac{\lambda_u}{N_u} \sum_{\boldsymbol{x}_i^u} P(j|\boldsymbol{x}_i^u) \right) \quad (5.3.10)
$$

$$
\widehat{\boldsymbol{\mu}}_j \;=\; \frac{\frac{\lambda_l}{N_l} \sum_{\boldsymbol{x}_i^l} \tau(j|\boldsymbol{x}_i^l)\boldsymbol{x}_i^l + \frac{\lambda_u}{N_u} \sum_{\boldsymbol{x}_i^u} P(j|\boldsymbol{x}_i^u)\boldsymbol{x}_i^u}{\frac{\lambda_l}{N_l} \sum_{\boldsymbol{x}_i^l} \tau(j|\boldsymbol{x}_i^l) + \frac{\lambda_u}{N_u} \sum_{\boldsymbol{x}_i^u} P(j|\boldsymbol{x}_i^u)} \quad (5.3.11)
$$

$$
\widehat{\boldsymbol{\Sigma}}_j = \frac{\frac{\lambda_l}{N_l} \sum_{\boldsymbol{x}_i^l} \tau(j|\boldsymbol{x}_i^l)(\boldsymbol{x}_i^l - \widehat{\boldsymbol{\mu}}_j)(\boldsymbol{x}_i^l - \widehat{\boldsymbol{\mu}}_j)^T + \frac{\lambda_u}{N_u} \sum_{\boldsymbol{x}_i^u} P(j|\boldsymbol{x}_i^u)(\boldsymbol{x}_i^u - \widehat{\boldsymbol{\mu}}_j)(\boldsymbol{x}_i^u - \widehat{\boldsymbol{\mu}}_j)^T}{\frac{\lambda_l}{N_l} \sum_{\boldsymbol{x}_i^l} \tau(j|\boldsymbol{x}_i^l) + \frac{\lambda_u}{N_u} \sum_{\boldsymbol{x}_i^u} P(j|\boldsymbol{x}_i^u)},
$$
$$
(5.3.12)
$$

where $\boldsymbol{x}_i^l \in \boldsymbol{x}_i \in \mathcal{D}_\ell$ and $\boldsymbol{x}_i^u \in \boldsymbol{x}_i \in \mathcal{D}_u$. The complete algorithm of the semi-supervised learning using regularized weighting factors is presented in Algorithm 8.

5.4   Experimental Results

In order to fundamentally understand the behavior of unlabeled data for classification, a series of experiments have been conducted. The objective

---

Algorithm 8 Semi-supervised learning using regularized weighting factors

---

1. **Input:** Training data set $\mathcal{D} = \mathcal{D}_\ell \cup \mathcal{D}_u$, weighting factors λ_l and λ_u. [MULTIPLE]: a set of labeled mixture components $\{(j, \mathbf{t}_j)|j = 1, ..., M\}$

2. **Initialize:** Model parameters $\mathbf{\Psi}^{(0)}$, component memberships $P(j|\mathbf{x})^{(0)}$ computed using $\mathbf{\Psi}^{(0)}$.

3. **Do for** $t = 0, ..., t_m$

   (a) E-Step: Evaluate the expectation of log-likelihood $\mathcal{Q}(\mathbf{\Psi}; \mathbf{\Psi}^{(t)})$ as in (5.2.8) by computing the constrained component memberships $P(j|\mathbf{x}_i)$ using current parameters $\mathbf{\Psi}^{(t)}$ as in Eq. (5.2.13)

   $$P(j|\mathbf{x}_i)^{(t+1)} = \begin{cases} z_{ji}, & \mathbf{x}_i \in \mathcal{D}_\ell \\ \dfrac{\pi_j^{(t)} p_j(\mathbf{x}_i|\boldsymbol{\theta}_j^{(t)})}{\sum_{j=1}^{c} \pi_j^{(t)} p_j(\mathbf{x}_i|\boldsymbol{\theta}_j^{(t)})}, & \mathbf{x}_i \in \mathcal{D}_u \end{cases}$$

   (b) [MULTIPLE]: For all labeled data $\mathbf{x}_i \in \mathcal{D}_l$, compute the restricted component memberships $\tau(j|\mathbf{x}_i)^{(t+1)}$ as in Eq. (5.2.19) using $P(j|\mathbf{x}_i)^{(t+1)}$

   (c) M-Step: Maximize the expectation $\mathcal{Q}(\mathbf{\Psi}; \mathbf{\Psi}^{(t)})$ formulated in (5.3.5) for simple models and (5.3.9) for complex models with multiple component per class by estimating $\mathbf{\Psi}^{(t+1)}$ given $P(j|\mathbf{x}_i)^{(t+1)}$ and $\tau(j|\mathbf{x}_i)^{(t+1)}$ (for [MULTIPLE] only) using upgrade equations (5.3.6), (5.3.7) and (5.3.8) for simple models and using (5.3.10), (5.3.11) and (5.3.12) for [MULTIPLE].

4. **Break if** $|\Delta\mathcal{L}| \leq \epsilon$, ϵ is an arbitrary small constant.

5. **Output:** Parameter estimate $\mathbf{\Psi}$.

---

of the experiments is to explore the following aspects. First, the effect of unlabeled data over model complexity. For this purpose we considered models with correct and incorrect structure. Second, to observe classifiers under overfitting, can unlabeled data help to avoid overfitting. Third, to observe effect of regularization using regularized weighting factors as introduced in section 5.3. Furthermore, we separated our results into two parts: experimental results without regularization and with regularization (using weighting factors).

For all experiment, we used EM algorithm with a common stopping condition. The iterations will be stopped when the change in log-likelihood from one iteration to the next fell below 10^{-5}. For all methods EM was initialized using the K-means given the labeled data only. The means parameters are initialized as the centroid of the Voronoi regions found. The variance parameters are initialized as the variances corresponding to the data in the Voronoi regions. The means of the K-means were initialized at random selected from the labeled data.

Data sets: We created two synthetic data sets of two-dimensions and two-classes: 2GAUSS and PARACHUTE data set. Class labels are balanced, half for each class. 2GAUSS data set is generated from two normal densities with the same spherical covariances. We generated 100 training sets with 4000 data points for each set and 100 test sets with 2000 data points not presented to the learning algorithm. In PARACHUTE data sets, the data are generated by ten gaussians, five gaussian densities for each class with the same variances. For training, 100 training sets are generated with 10000 data points for each set. We generated also 100 test data sets with 2000 data points to test the generalization of classifiers. The illustration of the data sets are as in Figure 5.1.

In the figures below, we evaluated the generalization error of classifiers (in percentage) provided by the different number of unlabeled data. After training of a classifier on the combined labeled and unlabeled training set, the test set is classified. We used new unlabeled examples to augment an existing training data set. For all experiments, we plot the average of test errors and their variance obtained from 100 independent trials for increased different number of unlabeled data. Experiments are also conducted for more complex models which use different number of mixture component per class. For convenient, we use notation of $M[m_1, m_2]$ for a model with M components mixture, m_1 components of class C_1 and m_2

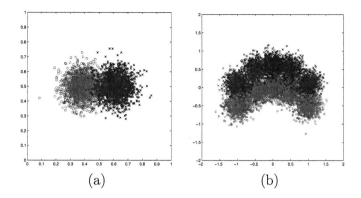

Figure 5.1: Plot of training data sets. Data points of the same class are shown using the same color. (a) 2GAUSS data set generated from two gaussian densities, $M = 2[1, 1]$, with the same variance. (b) PARACHUTE data set, each class was generated from five gaussian densities, $M = 10[5, 5]$, with the same variance.

components of class C_2.

5.4.1 Experiments Without Weighting Factors

In the following experiment we observed the effect of unlabeled data over performance of classification without regularization. In this scenario the contribution of labeled and unlabeled data are determined only by the size of the data. We conducted several experiments using PARACHUTE and 2GAUSS data sets and generative classifiers with different complexity, both correct and incorrect structure.

Experiments using correct models: For the first experiment, we used PARACHUTE data set and classifiers with *correct* models. The amount of labeled training data are varied. The result is presented in Figure 5.2. From the figure we learn that the unlabeled data can significantly help

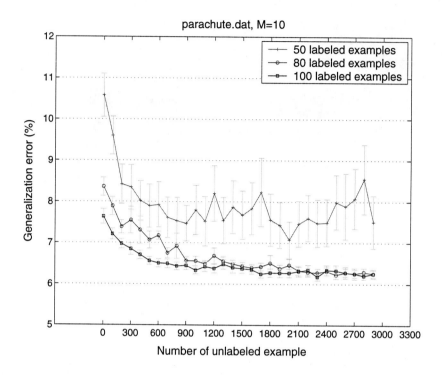

Figure 5.2: Generalization error of classifiers using PARACHUTE data set and correct models ($M = 10[5,5]$). Experiments used different number of labeled data points: 50, 80, and 100. **Horizontal axis**: amount of unlabeled data used. **Vertical-axis**: generalization error of classifiers. Error bars represent one standard error of the mean.

classification. This result is consistent with results as reported by authors in (Shahshahani & Landgrebe, 1994; Nigam *et al.*, 2000; Baluja, 1998; Cozman & Cohen, 2001). This result also favors the theoretical analysis of (Castelli & Cover, 1996) that unlabeled data can always help when the classifiers are unbiased. We observed also as in the figure, the variances of error are high when small labeled data are used for training in comparing with experiments using larger size of labeled data. Moreover, using correct models a degradation phenomena of classification performance did not observed.

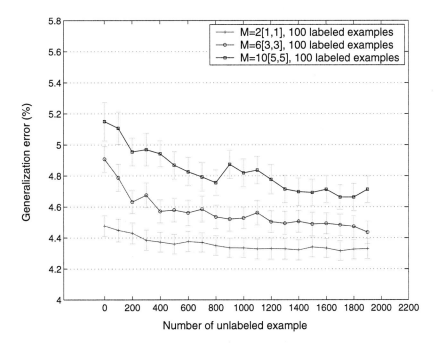

Figure 5.3: Generalization error of classifier trained using 2GAUSS data set with different model complexity. **Horizontal axis**: amount of unlabeled data used. **Vertical-axis**: generalization error. Error bars represent one standard error of the mean. Experiments were conducted using different number of mixture components per class: $2[1,1]$ (correct model), $6[3,3]$, and $10[5,5]$. All experiments used 100 labeled data points.

Experiments using incorrect models: To study the effect of model complexity, we varied the number of mixture components of the generative models. The experiments aim to answer the question whether the unlabeled data can help classification when the generative models are *incorrect*. The experiments were conducted using both 2GAUSS and PARACHUTE data set and the results are presented in Figure 5.3 and Figure 5.4, respectively.

In Figure 5.3 we can see that unlabeled data can improve classification performance for all classifiers with different model complexity, both correct model and incorrect models. We observed that unlabeled data can *always* help classification, not only when the models are correct but also when the models are incorrect.

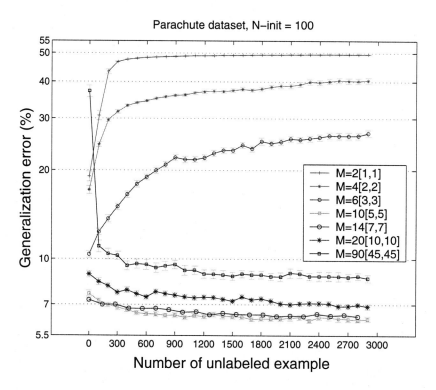

Figure 5.4: Generalization error of classifier trained using PARACHUTE data set with different model complexity. **Horizontal axis**: amount of unlabeled data used. **Vertical-axis**: generalization error. Error bars represent one standard error of the mean. Experiments were conducted using different number of mixture components per class: $2[1,1]$, $4[2,2]$, $6[3,3]$, $10[5,5]$ (correct model), $14[7,7]$, $20[10,10]$ and $90[45,45]$. All experiments used 100 labeled data points.

In Figure 5.4 we investigated mixture models trained using PARACHUTE data set with different model complexity. To avoid singularities during EM training, especially when the models are very complex with a large number of components, we applied a regularization method of the maximum penalized likelihood approach (Ormoneit & Tresp, 1996) by choosing a penalty parameter ω_{Sigma} to a small constant, while the other parameters were set to zero.

Here, we observed some interesting results in which we found different effects of unlabeled data. First, unlabeled data can *improve* the performance when the generative models are enough to estimate underlying distribution of the data although the model is *incorrect* (see e.g. models with $M = 20[10, 10]$ and $M = 90[45, 45]$). Second, unlabeled data can improve classification performance when the classifiers under overfitting condition (see the figure, when the model consists of $M = 90[45, 45]$ component densities). This result also emphasizes that unlabeled data can help classification although classifiers are build using incorrect models. Third, we observed however that unlabeled data *can degrade* performance of classification when the generative models are built using incorrect structures which are not enough to estimate the underlying distribution. This degradation phenomena is consistent with previous results (Cozman & Cohen, 2001; Baluja, 1998; Nigam *et al.*, 2000).

5.4.2 Experiments With Weighting Factors

In the following experiments we used the proposed regularization method, in which the log-likelihood are weighted using regularized weighting factors to adjust the strength of contribution of labeled/unlabeled data as discussed in Section 5.3. For all experiments we set the weighting factor of labeled data to a constant value (here $\lambda_l = 1$) and varied the weighting factor of unlabeled data (λ_u). Then, performance of classifiers were observed for different model complexity, both correct and incorrect structure.

Experiment using correct models: We considered effect of weighting factors to regularize contribution of unlabeled data when the generative models have correct structure. Empirical study was performed using 2GAUSS and PARACHUTE data set. Using 2GAUSS data set the result of the experiment can be seen in Figure 5.5a, in which the weighting factor of unlabeled data λ_u are varied, while weighting factor of labeled data was set to a same constant value, $\lambda_l = 1$. Here, we can learn that by using the correct model the weighted unlabeled data can always improve performance of classification. Generally, for correct models a large weighting value of unlabeled data gives an optimal performance of the classifier.

The similar results also were observed by using PARACHUTE data in Figure 5.6c. Using correct models the weighted unlabeled data generally increase performance of the classifiers. The figure also show us how weighting factors influenced performance of the classifiers and more robust to the different number of data. We can see when a weighting factor of unlabeled data was set to a small value, e.g. $\lambda_u = 0.2(\lambda_u < \lambda_l)$, the *asymptotical* value of classification error increase, so that the unlabeled data improved with only small increasing of the performance. However, when the unlabeled data are weighted by large values ($\lambda_u = 2.0$ and 5.0), dramatically decreased the asymptotic of classification error. It is also interesting to observe that in this particular case, large size of unlabeled data are necessary to achieve the asymptotic values. For example, as showed in the figure by using $\lambda_u = 5.0$ we need only 1500 unlabeled examples to achieve asymptotic value, while about 1200 unlabeled examples to achieve an asymptotic using $\lambda_u = 1$.

Experiments using incorrect models: Experimental results using incorrect models are represented in some figures as follows. For 2GAUSS data set the experimental results are represented in Figure 5.5b and 5.5c, while for PARACHUTE data set in Figure 5.6a, 5.6b and 5.6d.

Using 2GAUSS data set, an improvement of classification performance by augmenting unlabeled data was observed although models have incorrect structure (see 5.5b and 5.5c). When the generative model is incorrect and too weak in comparing with the correct model (see for $M = 10[5, 5]$), however, poor performance of the classifier was observed (in comparing with the other models) as showed in Figure 5.5c. Nevertheless, we can still observe improvement of the classifiers by weighting unlabeled data with a large weighting factor (Figure 5.5c for $\lambda_u = 5.0$).

An interesting result can be seen in figure 5.6 when experiments were performed using PARACHUTE data set. From the figure we can learn that by using incorrect models, the weighted unlabeled data do *not always* improve classification performance. Figure 5.6a and 5.6b show that the weighted unlabeled data can *degrade* performance of the classifiers when structure of the models have components $M = 2[1, 1]$ and $6[3, 3]$. In Figure 5.6d, however, weighted unlabeled data can improve performance although the classifier was built using *incorrect* model but enough to represent the underlying distribution.

5.5 Conclusion

In this chapter we studied semi-supervised learning for generative classifiers based on gaussian mixture models, in which the classifiers are trained not only using labeled data but also unlabeled data. Our research primarily more interested in investigating effects of unlabeled data augmented to training data set when only small number of labeled data is available.

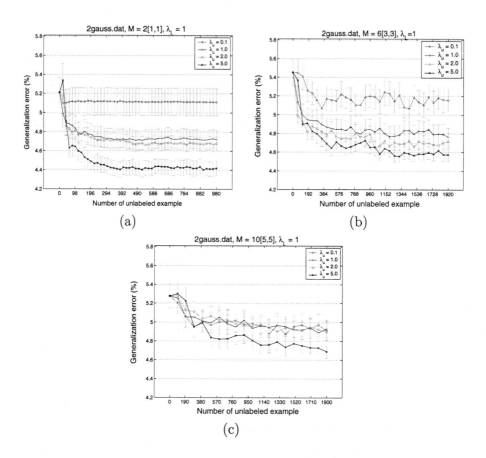

Figure 5.5: Performance of classifiers with different model complexity when 2GAUSS data set and the regularized weighting factors are used. The weighting factor of unlabeled data was varied to the values: λ_u = 0.1, 1.0, 2.0, and 5.0, while weighting factor of labeled data is set to one (λ_l = 1). **Horizontal-axis**: amount of unlabeled data used. **Vertical-axis**: generalization error. Error bars represent one standard error of the mean. Some experiments were conducted for different model complexity: (a) $M = 2[1,1]$ (**correct model**) with 20 labeled examples; (b) $M = 6[3,3]$ with 60 labeled examples; (c) $M = 10[5,5]$ with 100 labeled examples. Here the size of labeled data was set 10 labeled data points for one component.

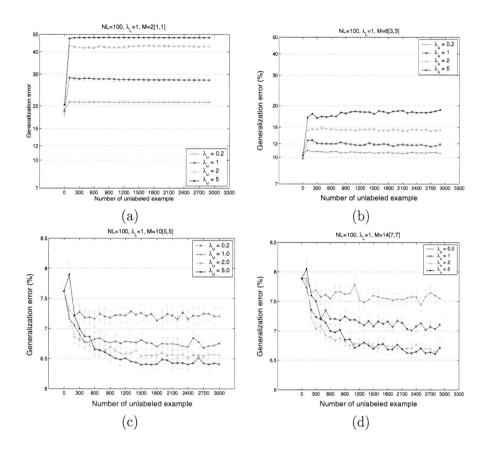

Figure 5.6: Performance of classifiers with different model complexity when PARACHUTE data set and the regularized weighting factors are used. The weighting factor of unlabeled data was varied to the values: $\lambda_u =$ 0.1, 1.0, 2.0, and 5.0, while weighting factor of labeled data is set to one ($\lambda_l = 1$). **Horizontal-axis**: amount of unlabeled data used. **Vertical-axis**: generalization error. Error bars represent one standard error of the mean. Some experiments were conducted for different model complexity: (a) $M = 2[1,1]$, (b) $M = 6[3,3]$, (c) $M = 10[5,5]$ (**correct model**), (d) $M = 14[7,7]$. For all experiments were conducted using 100 labeled data points.

In this chapter we presented a detailed analysis on this effect. In order to regularize the contribution of unlabeled data we proposed a method by weighting the terms of log-likelihood with weighting factors. The weighting factors are to modulate to which EM weights unlabeled data.

Our research is devoted to explore a basic question: under which conditions unlabeled data can help classification? Although some authors in the literature have investigated this theme in long time some questions remain unclear. Furthermore, our research was devoted to explore some aspects. First, the effect of the unlabeled data on the model complexity. We considered the effect for different model complexity including correct structure and incorrect structure. Second, the effect of unlabeled data on overfitting condition. Special attention is given to observe, if unlabeled data can help to avoid overfitting. Finally, we presented a regularization method to adjust the strength of labeled/unlabeled data's contribution. For this case we proposed a novel method by weighting the log-likelihood using the *regularized* weighting factors. This method is useful when full complexity of data sets cannot be completely captured by mixture models. By adjusting the weighting parameter of unlabeled data an optimal classifier can be found.

From the performed experiments some results were found. First, we observed that unlabeled data can *always* help classification when a generative model has a *correct* structure. Indeed, a high performance can be achieved by augmenting a large number of unlabeled data. The results of empirical study also showed that labeled data play important role in reducing bias and variance of the generalization error. This result is consistent with results as reported in (Shahshahani & Landgrebe, 1994; Baluja, 1998; Nigam *et al.*, 2000; Cozman *et al.*, 2003). In the other condition, however, the unlabeled data *can not always* help classification, especially when the generative models have *incorrect* structure. We observed that the unlabeled data can improve performance a classifier build using incorrect structure when the number of mixture components enough to represent the underlying distribution. When the generative models were constructed using a few mixture components and not enough to represent the underlying distribution a degradation phenomena was observed. An interesting result was observed that the unlabeled data can help to avoid overfitting condition. These results emphasizes that unlabeled data can help classification although classifiers are build using incorrect models, even when learning system reaches overfitting condition.

The similar phenomena also are observed when our regularization method is applied. Using correct models the *weighted* unlabeled data can also always help classification. Degradation phenomena caused by weighted unlabeled data also is observed in the experimental results when classifiers are built using incorrect models with structure not enough to model data distribution. Using the method, classifiers will achieve certain level of asymptotic values of classification error. When the correct models are used, high performance can be achieved by setting weighting factor of unlabeled data with a large value. In contrast, when the generative models are incorrect and the structure of the models not enough to model data distribution, the unlabeled data degrade performance. From the conducted experiments, the proposed regularization method can be used to control the strength of contribution of labeled/unlabeled data.

CHAPTER 6

Active Learning for Mixture Model-based Classifiers

In Chapter 5 we discussed learning algorithms that aim to reduce the number of labeled data by taking advantage of unlabeled data to improve performance of classifiers. The training data are gathered by sampling at *random* from an underlying distribution then a part of them is labeled according to the class labels. Learners do not have power to control over information that it receives and accepts whatever training examples are given to them. This learning framework is called *passive learning*. In this chapter we will study another framework of machine learning so-called *active learning* (Cohn *et al.*, 1994; Mitchell, 1997). In this framework the learner itself is responsible for acquiring the training examples, so that it can carefully select examples to be labeled. With this additional power it is expected that high performance of classifiers can be reached using small size of labeled data.

Active learning methods are very important in many practical setting, since procuring class labels can be costly and time-consuming. For example, in domains such as remote sensing data and medical image we require expensive human expertise for labeling each example of the data. In other domains such as speech- and character-recognition, text and web documents, the labeling may be time-consuming and need high patient. Comparing with passive learning systems, active learning systems demonstrated a significant decrease in the number of labeled example required to achieve a particular level of classifier performance.

6.1 What is Active Learning?

Active learning is also called *query* learning (Angluin, 1988). It concentrates on algorithms for identification of target concepts. Typically, an active learning method consists of two parts: a training and a query algorithm as in Algorithm 9. A learner first is trained with very small number of labeled examples selected at random or provided by an oracle, an expert that can label any input data without error. Query algorithm is then used to select carefully a new additional example by asking queries and receiving responses. The responses are measured using certain criterion that are usually determined using the selected examples so far. The measure of the responses describes quality of queries. A most informative example, i.e. resulting optimal response respect to the criterion, will be selected and requested to the oracle for labeling, before being added to the training data set. Training algorithm is run again, new querying begins and so on. This learning process is repeated until certain number of query or satisfactory performance is met.

Recently, numerous methods of active learning have been proposed

---

Algorithm 9 General approach of active learning

---

1. **Input:** A set of unlabeled examples. Number of request N_{req}.

2. **Initialize:** A few number of training examples

3. **Do for** $t < N_{req}$

   (a) **Query**: Select an unlabeled example for querying and update the training set

   (b) **Training**: Update classifier using the current training set

4. **Return:** Trained classifier

---

in the literature. Generally, the methods can be categorized into two different approaches. The first attaints optimal solution based on a statistically optimal solution, while the second optimizes the other criterion in order to maximize expected error reduction, e.g. by minimizing the size of the version space (Seung *et al.*, 1992; Tong & Koller, 2001b).

A method belongs to the first approach was proposed by Cohn et al in (Cohn *et al.*, 1995). They proposed a method by choosing queries that minimize the learner variance when the queries to be labeled and added to the training data. Assuming that learner is unbiased, then the reduction of the learner variance will directly maximize the error reduction (Geman *et al.*, 1992). The method was developed and applied to the regression problems using statistical models (Cohn *et al.*, 1995). Unfortunately, this approach needs a closed form calculation of the expected learner's variance which is impracticable for arbitrary classifiers and difficult to solve. This problem was also informed by some authors e.g. in (Roy & McCallum, 2001; Maram *et al.*, 2004; Saar-Tsechansky & Provost, 2004).

Most active learning methods in the literature use the second approach. Here we consider three important methods. First is *Query-by-Committee* (QBC) algorithm introduced by Seung et al (Seung *et al.*, 1992). The algorithm uses the size of *version space* (Mitchel, 1982), i.e.

the subset of parameter space that consistent to the current training examples, as a utility measure to be minimized. The algorithm employs a committee of learners sampled from the current version space to decide an example whether or not to request its label. The example is selected according to the principle of maximum disagreement among committee members regarding its class prediction. In (Freund *et al.*, 1997), authors proved effectiveness of QBC in decreasing the prediction error rapidly with the number of queries. The QBC works on the stream-based learning.

Second method was proposed by Tong & Koller (Tong & Koller, 2001b) for Support Vector Machines (SVMs). Here we call the method as active-SVMs. The method is based on the similar criterion as in QBC, namely reducing the version space size. They used the size of version space as a quality criterion of queries. The method works under the pool-based learning, in which learner has access to a pool of unlabeled example. Using this criterion the current SVMs classifier will choose an example from the pool closest to the decision hyperplane in kernel space. They applied this method for text classification (Tong & Koller, 2001b) and image retrieval task (Tong & Chang, 2001).

The Query by Committee and active-SVMs methods above, however, impose strictly requirements assuming that a perfect deterministic classifier exists. In the real world, however, these assumptions are problematic and difficult to be satisfied (Lewis & Gale, 1994; Roy & McCallum, 2001). An alternative method called the *uncertainty sampling* method have been presented by Lewis & Gale (Lewis & Gale, 1994). The algorithm selects iteratively an example from a pool of unlabeled example with greatest uncertainty in predicted class membership. This is a heuristic method which efficiently in searching informative queries. Unfortunately it doest not converge to the optimal classifier quickly in comparing with QBC as informed by Freund et al in (Freund *et al.*, 1997). Essentially, the three proposed active learning methods, the uncertainty sampling, QBC and active-SVMs, choose informative examples which have the highest uncertainty of class label (Tong & Chang, 2001).

Most of proposed methods in the literature tend to choose examples that close to the decision boundaries and give no attention to the prior data distribution. An analysis on this theme was given by Zang & Oles in (Zhang & Oles, 2000). They noted that the existing active learning algorithms are more suitable for discriminative models in which the model parameter is not for the purpose of generating the class members, but rather for discriminating in-class members from out-of-class members.

Currently, some authors e.g. in (McCallum & Nigam, 1998; Nguyen & Smeulders, 2004) developed new methods that take the prior data distribution into account to achieve better performance of probabilistic classifiers. In (McCallum & Nigam, 1998) a Naive Bayes classifiers are trained over both labeled and unlabeled examples using EM algorithm. They modified Query By Committee algorithm (Seung *et al.*, 1992) by weighting the uncertainty measure with the density of the samples. Since the Naive Bayes classifier is a generative classifier for which training relies on the estimation of the class-conditional densities, the estimation using QBC is inaccurate. The chosen examples are closest to the current classification boundary, which not represent the actual data distribution as criticized in (Nguyen & Smeulders, 2004; Seeger, 2001). In (Nguyen & Smeulders, 2004), the authors developed an algorithm by taking advantage of prior data distribution for *discriminative* classifiers based on the linear logistic regression.

In this chapter we present novel methods of active learning for the generative classifiers, especially for the classifiers based on mixture models. The proposed methods are the *Expected Likelihood-based Sampling* and

Likelihood-Increasing Sampling. These algorithms based on the likelihood as criterion in choosing queries to be labeled. The proposed methods attempt to find good performance of classifiers based on generative models built using as small number of labeled data as possible. These methods work under pool-based learning, in which learners have access to all possible queries.

The *Expected Likelihood-based Sampling* (ELS) use the expected likelihood as criterion to choose a new example for labeling iteratively. Each iteration consist of two parts: training and query phase. After training phase, a new example is selected for labeling from the pool of unlabeled examples with lowest expected likelihood. The expected likelihood is measured using current model and a new example added to the training set.

The *Likelihood-Increasing Sampling* (LIS) attempts to obtain representative examples whereby an optimal model can be constructed. The algorithm selects carefully a new example from a pool of unlabeled data that has largest contribution to the increasing of current likelihood. We use the pool of unlabeled data and collected labeled data to estimate the likelihood of the estimated model and determine the impact of each potential labeling request on the expected likelihood. In this chapter both ELS and LIS algorithm have been implemented using classifiers based on gaussian mixture models for binary classification problems.

6.2   Generative Classifiers: A Review

This section describes a generative classifier in which a Bayesian probabilistic framework used for classification. In the next two sections we present active learning methods by building on this framework. In this framework the data are assumed to be generated by a particular parametric model and use training data set to estimate the model parameter.

The generative model then is employed to construct a classifier by maximizing the posterior probability.

Let $P(C_k|\boldsymbol{x})$ be a posterior probability of class membership C_k. Through Bayes's theorem, the posterior probability can be expressed in the form

$$P(C_j|\boldsymbol{x}) = \frac{P(C_j)p(\boldsymbol{x}|C_j)}{\sum_{k=1}^{c} P(C_k)p(\boldsymbol{x}|C_k)}, \qquad (6.2.1)$$

where $P(C_k)$ is the prior probabilities and $p(\boldsymbol{x}|C_k)$ is the class-conditional densities. To classify a new example, we can use the optimal Bayesian decision rule. The rule minimizes the probability of misclassification by assigning an example $\boldsymbol{x}$ to a class C_k having the largest posterior probability

$$P(C_k|\boldsymbol{x}) > P(C_j|\boldsymbol{x}) \text{ for all } j \neq k. \qquad (6.2.2)$$

Let $f(\boldsymbol{x})$ be a classifier mapping input space $\mathcal{X}$ to the discrete output space $\mathcal{C}$: $f(\boldsymbol{x}) : \mathcal{X} \to \mathcal{C}$. The classifier can be expressed in the form

$$f(\boldsymbol{x}) = \arg \max_{C_k \in \mathcal{C}} P(C_k)p(\boldsymbol{x}|C_k). \qquad (6.2.3)$$

Under this framework, the problem of classification therefore can be regarded as class-conditional densities estimation problem, since the class-conditional densities determines the form of decision boundaries and performance of the classifiers.

In this chapter we consider the mixture models (McLachlan & Peel, 2000; Titterington *et al.*, 1985) to estimate the class-conditional densities. The mixture models represents a probability density function $p(\boldsymbol{x})$ as a linear combination of the finite component densities

$$p(\boldsymbol{x}|\boldsymbol{\Psi}) = \sum_{j=1}^{M} \pi_j p(\boldsymbol{x}|\theta_j), \qquad (6.2.4)$$

where M is the number of mixture components, $\boldsymbol{\Psi}$ is a vector of mixture parameters (π, θ), $p(\boldsymbol{x}|\theta_j)$ is the class-conditional density and π_j is the mixing coefficient. When the component densities are gaussians, the model parameter is represented by $\boldsymbol{\Psi} = (\pi, \boldsymbol{\mu}, \boldsymbol{\Sigma})$, where $\boldsymbol{\mu}$ and $\boldsymbol{\Sigma}$ are means and covariance parameter, respectively.

In the classification problem a set of labeled data $\mathcal{D} = \{(\boldsymbol{x}_1, \boldsymbol{z}_1), ..., (\boldsymbol{x}_N, \boldsymbol{z}_N)\}$ is given, where $\boldsymbol{z}_i$ is class label of input vector $\boldsymbol{x}_i$. Each class of the data can be represented by single mixture component (simple model) or multiple mixture components (complex model). The parameter of the model then can be estimated using the maximum-likelihood approach. For simple model the log-likelihood can be written in the form

$$\mathcal{L}(\mathcal{D}|\boldsymbol{\Psi}) = \sum_{k=1}^{c} \sum_{\boldsymbol{x} \in C_k} \ln \pi_k p(\boldsymbol{x}|\boldsymbol{\theta}_k), \qquad (6.2.5)$$

where c is the number of classes, C_k is a class and $p(\boldsymbol{x}|\boldsymbol{\theta}_k)$ represents the class-conditional density of class C_k. For complex models, each class of the data is represented by a mixture of several densities, so that $p(\boldsymbol{x}|\boldsymbol{\Psi})$ in (6.2.4) can be used to estimate a class-conditional density with M mixture components. Parameter of the model then can be estimated using EM algorithm as explained in Chapter 3 of this dissertation.

6.3 Active Leaning using Expected Likelihood-based Sampling

In this section we introduce an active learning method, we call the Expected Likelihood-based Sampling (ELS), that takes into account the prior data distribution to obtain good performance of generative classifiers using as small number of labeled data as possible. To obtain good models the method evaluates future likelihood by sampling a new example from a data pool to be added into training data set. Instead of choosing the example that results largest future likelihood, the algorithm selects the example that has the lowest contribution to the current likelihood. The

algorithm assumes that a pool of unlabeled data is available and estimates the future likelihood using expectation of the likelihood. Here, the
expected likelihood is measured using current model and a new example
added to the training data set. In this section we consider the classifiers
based on gaussians mixture models for binary classification problems.

The basic idea of the algorithm can be explained as follows. We
consider a binary classification problem and a simple model, in which
each class of training data is represented by single component of mixture.
It is fact that examples that closed to the center of a given kernel will give
high expected likelihood, while the examples that far away from the kernel
centers will give low expected likelihood. When we take a new example
with high expected likelihood, it will reinforce our belief on the current
model which typically weak. Our method, therefore, selects an example
from a pool of unlabeled examples with *lowest* expected-likelihood for
querying. The example selected using this criterion will avoid a learning
system from a local optimum of model estimation and speed up learning
system to reach robust model which cover entirely data distribution.

An illustration of the Expected-Likelihood-based Sampling algorithm
is given in the Figure 6.1. We consider in the simulation a binary classification problem and each class is represented by single component of
mixture with spherical covariance parameter. The query process is begun by employing a weak model initialized using a few number of labeled
examples. The examples with lowest expected likelihood will be chosen
to be labeled. From the figures can be seen, that the selected examples
spread out far from the centers of mixture components. The algorithm
can attaints a robust model after a few small number of queries, even
when the learning system is initialized using a weak model. The algorithm selects examples, whereby local optimum of model estimation can
be avoided and a good classifier can be obtained.

6.3.1   Description of Algorithm

The Expected Likelihood-based Sampling algorithm consist of two parts: training and query algorithm. The algorithm may begin with a weak model estimated using a small training set of N labeled examples sampled from a pool of unlabeled examples $\mathcal{P}$. The unlabeled examples define the examples we can query labels for. The algorithm proceeds by adding new labeled examples to the labeled training set, one at a time. In each iteration, it chooses an example from the data pool with the lowest expected likelihood. The selected example is queried the oracle for labeling. The algorithm stops when it has sufficiently many examples. The accumulated set of labeled examples then can be used to construct a generative classifier by employing the Bayes optimal decision rule.

We consider now a gaussian mixture model with M components, in which each component represents a class of the data. Let $\boldsymbol{\Psi}$ be the current model parameter estimated using training data set $\mathcal{D} = \{(\boldsymbol{x}_1, \boldsymbol{z}_1), ..., (\boldsymbol{x}_N, \boldsymbol{z}_N)\}$, where $\boldsymbol{z}_i$ is class label vector of $\boldsymbol{x}_i$ with $\boldsymbol{z}_i = (z_{i1}, ..., z_{iM})^T$ and $z_{ji} \in \{1, 0\}$ according to whether $\boldsymbol{x}_i$ is generated or not from component j of the mixture. The log-likelihood of labeled training data set then can be written in the form

$$\mathcal{L}(\mathcal{D}|\boldsymbol{\Psi}) = \sum_{\boldsymbol{x}_i \in \mathcal{D}} \sum_j z_{ji} \ln \pi_j p(\boldsymbol{x}_i|\boldsymbol{\theta}_j). \qquad (6.3.1)$$

In this simple case, π_j represents prior probability and $p(\boldsymbol{x}_i|\boldsymbol{\theta}_j)$ represents class-conditional density of class j.

Suppose $\boldsymbol{x}^*$ is a new example sampled from a pool of unlabeled examples $\mathcal{P}$. When $\boldsymbol{x}^*$ is added to the training data set $\mathcal{D}$, the expectation of the log-likelihood of the new training data set $\mathcal{D}^* = \{\mathcal{D} \cup \boldsymbol{x}^*\}$ can be

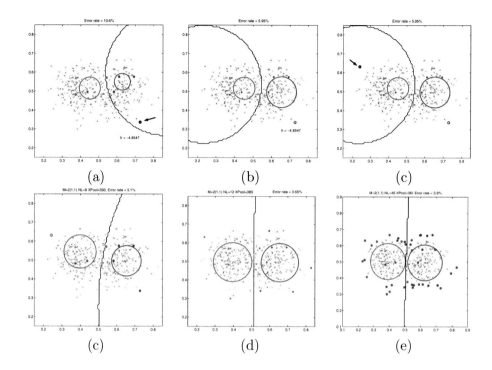

Figure 6.1: Illustration of query selections using the *Expected-Likelihood-based Sampling* (ELS) algorithm. (a) The query process is begun by employing a weak model initialized using six labeled examples. The arrow points to an informative example selected for querying from the pool according to the current model. (b) The selected query after labeling and added to training set for next queries. The new example expanded covariance of the gaussian (blue, right side). (c) The model after two new examples added to the training set. The selected examples expanded covariance of both gaussians, so that the model covers the data set. The graph of (d) and (e) show the distribution of selected examples, centers and covariance of the gaussians after 6 and 34 queries, respectively. An interesting graph is shown in (d), in which a perfect decision boundary (black line) was achieved using only six queries.

written in the form

$$\mathcal{E}_z[\mathcal{L}(\mathcal{D}^*|\mathbf{\Psi})] = \mathcal{E}_z[\mathcal{L}(\mathcal{D}|\mathbf{\Psi})] + \sum_j P(j|\boldsymbol{x}^*)\ln \pi_j p(\boldsymbol{x}^*|\theta_j). \qquad (6.3.2)$$

The expected log-likelihood (6.3.2) is used as criterion for query selection of our algorithm. Since the expected log-likelihood of the labeled data set is fixed, not depend on the considering example $\boldsymbol{x}^*$, therefore, it is sufficient to consider the second term of (6.3.2) as a selection criterion

$$\mathcal{E}_z[\mathcal{L}(\boldsymbol{x}^*|\boldsymbol{\Psi})] = \sum_j P(j|\boldsymbol{x}^*) \ln \pi_j p(\boldsymbol{x}^*|\theta_j). \qquad (6.3.3)$$

After training phase given training data set, query selection can be done by assigning every example $\boldsymbol{x}$ in the data pool $\mathcal{P}$ by a score of the expectation (6.3.3). The algorithm then selects an potential example $\boldsymbol{x}^*$ with the lowest expected log-likelihood in comparing with all examples in the pool

$$\arg \min_{\boldsymbol{x} \in \mathcal{P}} \mathcal{E}_z[\mathcal{L}(\boldsymbol{x}|\boldsymbol{\Psi})], \qquad (6.3.4)$$

where the model parameter $\boldsymbol{\Psi}$ is estimated using current training data set $\mathcal{D}$ by employing EM algorithm. Complete the Expected Likelihood-based Sampling algorithm is presented in Algorithm 10

6.3.2   Experimental Results

We evaluate the performance of the **ELS** algorithm on the artificial and benchmark data sets from UCI repository (Blake & Merz, 1998). The artificial data sets are BANANA, HEART and DIABETES of benchmark collections selected and used by Rätsch et al. in (Rätsch *et al.*, 2001). The HEART and DIABETES data set are extracted from UCI repository. All data sets are binary classification problems. The HEART data set contains 170 examples of 13-dimensions, while DIABETES data set contains 468 examples of 8-dimensions. For visualization purposes we created also a two-dimension artificial data set, namely 2GAUSS data set.

Algorithm 10 Active learning using Expected Likelihood-based Sampling (ELS)

---

1. **Input:** Pool of unlabeled examples $\mathcal{P} = \{\mathbf{x}_1, ..., \mathbf{x}_N\}$. Number of request N_{req}.

2. **Initialize:** Lebeled data set $\mathcal{D} = \{(\mathbf{x}_1, \mathbf{z}_1), ..., (\mathbf{x}_{N_l}, \mathbf{z}_{N_l})\}$ selected at random from $\mathcal{P}$, $\mathbf{z}_i = \text{oracle}(\mathbf{x}_i)$, $\mathcal{P} \leftarrow \{\mathcal{P} \backslash \mathcal{D}\}$

3. **Do for** $t = 1, ..., N_{req}$

   (a) **Training**: Run EM to obtain model parameter $\mathbf{\Psi}^t$ given training set $\mathcal{D}$

   (b) **Query**:

      i. For each $\mathbf{x} \in \mathcal{P}$ assign to $\mathbf{x}$ the expected log-likelihood $\mathcal{E}_z[\mathcal{L}(\mathcal{D}^*|\mathbf{\Psi}^t)]$ using Eq. (6.3.2)

      ii. Select an example $\mathbf{x}^*$ for which $\mathcal{E}_z[\mathcal{L}(\mathcal{D}^*|\mathbf{\Psi}^t)]$ is lowest.

   (c) Update training set and data pool: $\mathcal{D} \leftarrow \{\mathcal{D} \cup (\mathbf{x}^*, \mathbf{z}^*)\}$, $\mathcal{P} \leftarrow \{\mathcal{P} \backslash \mathbf{x}^*\}$, where $\mathbf{z}^* = \text{oracle}(\mathbf{x}^*)$

4. **Return:** Model parameter $\mathbf{\Psi}$

For all problems this collection includes fixed 100 folds each consisting of fixed 60%/40% training/test replication. The experiments were performed using the Expected Likelihood-based Sampling method and random selection method. The results of experiments, the means and standard deviations of the average classification errors on the test sets are presented in Figure 6.4, 6.5 and 6.6.

In all experiments described below, each classifier was constructed using gaussian mixture models with spherical covariance parameter. We considered performance of classifiers built using different model complexity by using different number of mixture components to model class-conditional densities. The model structure is denoted by $M[m_1, m_2]$ to describe an model constructed using M component densities; m_1 components of class c_1 and m_2 components of class c_2.

Approximation of the model parameters were performed using EM algorithm. For all experiments K-means was applied to initialize EM.

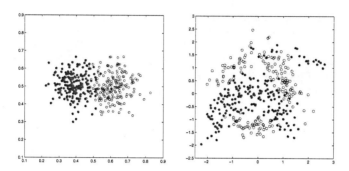

Figure 6.2: Two dimensional synthetic data sets. **Left**: 2GAUSS data set consisting of 400 data points. **Right**: BANANA consisting of 400 data points, has zero mean and standard deviation one.

The means and the covariance matrices are initialized as the centroid of the Voronoi sets found and the covariance matrices corresponding to the data in the Voronoi sets respectively. The mixing parameters of the mixture were initialized as the proportion of the examples present in each Voronoi sets. The prototypes of the K-means itself were initialized at random from the training data set.

We compare the *Expected Likelihood-based Sampling* - the method introduced in this section - choosing the examples that minimize the expected likelihood as in equation (6.3.2) with random sampling - choosing the query example at random. The result of experiments are presented in the graphs below.

In Figure 6.3 and 6.4 we depict the generalization error of the proposed active learning method and passive selection obtained on the artificial two-dimensional data sets, 2GAUSS and BANANA data set, respectively. For both data sets, the *Expected Likelihood-based Sampling* method significantly overcome the random selection. The the *Expected Likelihood-based Sampling* method show reducing classification error quickly

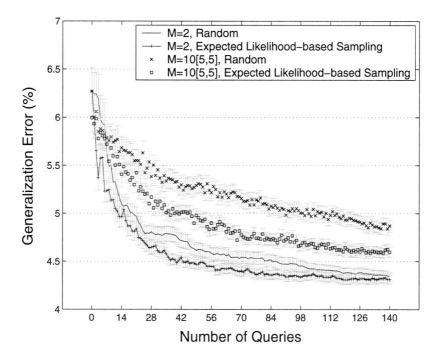

Figure 6.3: The result of experiment using the *Expected Likelihood-based Sampling* method using 2GAUSS data sets and a pool of 400 examples. **Horizontal-axis**: the number of queries. **Vertical-axis**: generalization error. Error bars represent one standard error of the mean. In this experiment, the classifiers were built using gaussian mixture models with different number of component densities: $M = 2[1, 1]$ and $10[5,5]$.

in compare to the passive method. For example, the the *Expected Likelihood-based Sampling* reaches mean about 12% error rate in 50 queries, while the passive method after choosing 155 queries. That means in this case the proposed method is 3.1 times faster than passive method to achieve the same level performance.

The results of experiments using HEART data set are as showed in Figure 6.5. The queries are selected randomly from 170 examples of

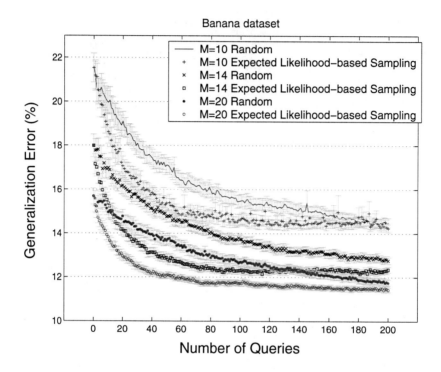

Figure 6.4: The result of experiment using the *Expected Likelihood-based Sampling* method using BANANA data sets and a pool of 400 examples. **Horizontal-axis**: the number of queries. **Vertical-axis**: generalization error. Error bars represent one standard error of the mean. In this experiment, the classifiers were built using gaussian mixture models with different number of component densities: $M = 2[1, 1]$, $14[7,7]$ and $20[10,10]$.

the pool data set. The *Expected Likelihood-based Sampling* method outperforms all three different complexity models with number of mixture components $2[1, 1], 4[2, 2]$ and $10[5, 5]$. The most significant improvement of the proposed method is observed in the figure with the $M = 4[2, 2]$ mixture components. On this structure the *Expected Likelihood-based Sampling* method demonstrated an significant reducing of labeled exam-

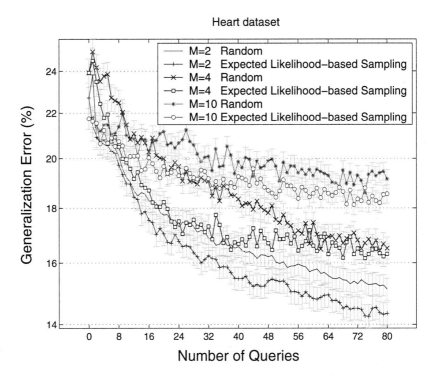

Figure 6.5: The result of experiment using the *Expected Likelihood-based Sampling* method and random selection on the HEART data set. The experiment was performed using a pool of unlabeled examples of 170 examples. **Horizontal-axis**: the number of queries. **Vertical-axis**: generalization error. Error bars represent one standard error of the mean. In this experiment, the classifiers were built using generative models with different number of component densities: $M = 2[1, 1], 4[2, 2]$ and $10[5,5]$.

ples to achieve the same level reached by random selection method. The proposed method reached error rate 18.0% only after 20 queries, where the same error was reached by passive method after 43 queries. That means the proposed method 2.15 times faster than passive learning method.

The result of experiment performed using DIABETES data set are as

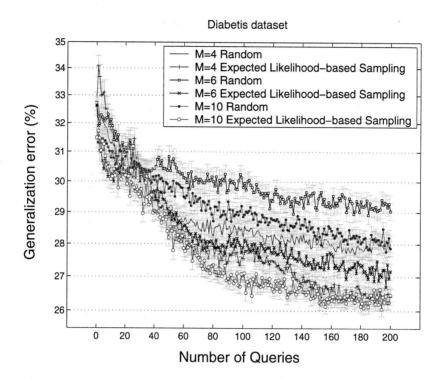

Figure 6.6: The result of experiment using the *Expected Likelihood-based Sampling* method and random selection on the DIABETES data set. The experiment was performed using a pool of unlabeled examples of 468 examples. **Horizontal-axis**: the number of queries. **Vertical-axis**: generalization error. Error bars represent one standard error of the mean. In this experiment, the classifiers were built using generative models with different number of component densities: $M = 4[2,2], 6[3,3]$ and $10[5,5]$.

presented in Figure 6.6. The DIABETES is 8-dimension data set contained 468 examples for two classes. This experiment trained the gaussian mixture models based classifiers to distinguish one class from the other class. The result of some experiments using this data set show that the *Expected Likelihood-based Sampling* method clearly outperforms the passive method, as shown in the figure. The proposed method also showed improving dramatically of classification performance using only small number of queries in comparing with random selection method. When we used model with $M = 10[5,5]$ mixture components, the *Expected Likelihood-based Sampling* method reached error rate 28.1% in 60 queries, while the same error was reached after 200 queries by random selection (passive method), or 3.3 times more slowly. The superior of the proposed method also was shown in the figure when $M = 6[3,3]$ mixture components was used to construct classifiers. The *Expected Likelihood-based Sampling* method reached error rate 29.2% using 48 labeled examples, while the passive method needed 180 labeled examples to achieve the same level. That mean the passive method is 3.75 time slowly.

6.3.3   Conclusion

In this section we presented an active learning method for classifiers based on mixture models. Unlike earlier works, the proposed method aims to reduce the number of labeled examples to obtain optimal models by choosing selectively new examples for labeling. The algorithm works under the pool-based learning, in which learners have access to all unlabeled example, and selects examples from the pool having the lowest expected likelihood. The expectation is evaluated using current model and an example candidate added to the training data set.

Some experiments have been performed to compare the performance of the proposed method and random selection method. The results of the performed experiments showed superiority of our method in improving performance of classifiers based on gaussian mixture models compared with passive learning method. The results of experiments using four data sets indicate that the proposed method dramatically reduced the number of labeled examples needed to achieve the same performance level of random selection method.

6.4 Active Leaning using Likelihood-Increasing Sampling

In the previous section we presented an active learning algorithm aim to find robust models by choosing training examples with lowest expected likelihood. The expectation is evaluated using current model and a new example added to the current training set. The algorithm heuristically seeks potential examples in the pool of unlabeled data to be labeled. The algorithm however should be employed carefully especially when the data is noisy.

In this section we introduce a novel active learning algorithm (we call the *Likelihood-Increasing Sampling*) that aims to obtain *representative* examples to build optimal generative models. This method attempts to achieve optimal models by choosing carefully queries iteratively. This method assumes a large pool of unlabeled examples be available. Here the likelihood is used as measure of the model quality. Therefore the method attempts to reach highest expected likelihood by evaluate a new example for all possible label. An example with highest average likelihood will be chosen for querying. To estimate the future likelihood the algorithm evaluates likelihood using current labeled training data set and unlabeled examples remain in the pool. By using this criterion, the method is more robust in handling noisy data.

6.4.1 Description of Algorithm

The learning problem of generative classifier is estimation of class-conditional densities given a set of labeled examples $\mathcal{D}_\ell$. In this chapter we consider the problem in which the class-conditional densities are estimated using the mixture models

$$p(\boldsymbol{x}|\boldsymbol{\Psi}) = \sum_{j=1}^{M} \pi_j p(\boldsymbol{x}|\boldsymbol{\theta}_j), \qquad (6.4.1)$$

where M is the number of mixture components and $\boldsymbol{\Psi}$ is a vector of mixture parameters $(\boldsymbol{\pi}, \boldsymbol{\theta})$. π_j are called the mixing coefficients and $p(\boldsymbol{x}|\boldsymbol{\theta}_j)$ are the component densities. Each class of the data can be represented by single mixture component (simple model) or multiple mixture components (complex model). The parameter of the model then can be estimated using the maximum-likelihood approach.

For simple model the log-likelihood can be written in the form

$$\mathcal{L}(\mathcal{D}|\boldsymbol{\Psi}) = \sum_{k=1}^{c} \sum_{\boldsymbol{x} \in C_k} \ln \pi_k p(\boldsymbol{x}|\boldsymbol{\theta}_k), \qquad (6.4.2)$$

where c is the number of classes, C_k is a class and $p(\boldsymbol{x}|\boldsymbol{\theta}_k)$ represents the class-conditional density of class C_k. For complex models, each class of the data is represented by a mixture of several densities, so that $p(\boldsymbol{x}|\boldsymbol{\Psi})$ in (6.4.1) can be used to estimate a class-conditional density with M mixture components. Parameter of the model then can be estimated using EM algorithm as explained in Chapter 3.

In the pool based active learning, a pool of unlabeled data $\mathcal{P}$ is available and a very small size of labeled data set $\mathcal{D}$ sampled at random from the pool is labeled to initialize the learning system. The goal of the active learning is to achieve high performance of the classifier using as small number of labeled data as possible by choosing carefully new examples for labeling. Let $\mathcal{D}$ is the labeled data set, the active learning algorithm chooses new examples from remaining unlabeled examples in the pool, $\mathcal{P} \leftarrow \{\mathcal{P} \backslash \mathcal{D}\}$.

In order to construct generative classifiers based on mixture models, the proposed active learning algorithm, the *Likelihood-Increasing Sampling*, attempts to choose representative examples from the pool for labeling so that the collected labeled examples can be used to construct an optimal model. In this algorithm we take a sampling approach to the likelihood and choice of query. Since the class labels of the data set before querying is unknown, we estimate future likelihood over the remaining unlabeled data in the pool $\mathcal{P}$ and the collected labeled samples $\mathcal{D}_\ell$ as follows

$$\mathcal{L}(\mathcal{U}|\boldsymbol{\Psi}) = \sum_{\boldsymbol{x}\in\mathcal{D}} \ln p(\boldsymbol{x}|\boldsymbol{\Psi}) + \sum_{\boldsymbol{x}\in\mathcal{P}} \ln p(\boldsymbol{x}|\boldsymbol{\Psi}), \qquad (6.4.3)$$

where $\mathcal{U} = \mathcal{D} \cup \mathcal{P}$.

The Likelihood-Increasing Sampling algorithm aims to choose a query, $\boldsymbol{x}^*$, such that when the query is given label $\boldsymbol{z}^*$ and added to the training set, the learner trained on the resulting set $\{\mathcal{D} \cup (\boldsymbol{x}^*, \boldsymbol{z}^*)\}$ has higher likelihood than any other $\boldsymbol{x}$. For a candidate example $\boldsymbol{x}^*$ sampled from $\mathcal{P}$, the query algorithm evaluates the expected log-likelihood over all possible class labels as follows.

First, the learner is trained using EM algorithm given the new training set $\{\mathcal{D} \cup (\boldsymbol{x}^*, \boldsymbol{z}^*)\}$ for all possible class labels $\boldsymbol{z}^* \in \mathcal{C}$. After EM is run on the new training data set for all possible labels of $\boldsymbol{x}^*$, we get a set of model parameter estimations $\{\hat{\boldsymbol{\Psi}}_{\mathcal{D}\cup(\boldsymbol{x}^*,\boldsymbol{z}^*)}|\boldsymbol{z}^* \in \mathcal{C}\}$. Furthermore we write $\mathcal{D} \cup (\boldsymbol{x}^*, \boldsymbol{z}^*)$ as $\mathcal{D}^*$ and $\hat{\boldsymbol{\Psi}}_{\mathcal{D}\cup(\boldsymbol{x}^*,\boldsymbol{z}^*)}$ as $\hat{\boldsymbol{\Psi}}_{\mathcal{D}^*}$. The log-likelihood of each estimated parameter $\hat{\boldsymbol{\Psi}}_{\mathcal{D}^*}$ can be written in the form

$$\widetilde{\mathcal{L}}(\mathcal{U}|\hat{\boldsymbol{\Psi}}_{\mathcal{D}^*}) = \mathcal{L}(\mathcal{D}|\hat{\boldsymbol{\Psi}}_{\mathcal{D}^*}) + \mathcal{L}(\mathcal{P}|\hat{\boldsymbol{\Psi}}_{\mathcal{D}^*}). \qquad (6.4.4)$$

Second, the expected log-likelihood is then computed as the average of the log-likelihoods using parameters resulted in the first step above (6.4.4) as follows

$$\mathcal{E}_z[\widetilde{\mathcal{L}}(\mathcal{U}|\hat{\boldsymbol{\Psi}}_{\mathcal{D}^*})] = \frac{1}{|\mathcal{C}|} \sum_{z^*\in\mathcal{C}} \widetilde{\mathcal{L}}(\mathcal{D}|\hat{\boldsymbol{\Psi}}_{\mathcal{D}^*}). \qquad (6.4.5)$$

Furthermore, the algorithm uses the expected log-likelihood as a criterion for selecting the queries. The query with highest the expected log-likelihood will be selected to be labeled and added into training set for next training process.

The complete algorithm of this method is presented in Algorithm 11. As an illustration how the algorithm chooses training data can be seen in the Figure 6.7. The figure shows the distribution of selected data that represent each cluster of the data. This is different with the previous proposed method (**ELS**) in which the selected data distribution spread far from the centers of gaussians.

Algorithm 11 Active learning using Likelihood-Increasing Sampling (**LIS**)

---

1. **Input:** Data pool $\mathcal{P}$, number of request N_{req}, initial training data $\mathcal{D}$, $\mathcal{P} \leftarrow \{\mathcal{P}\backslash\mathcal{D}\}$.

2. **Do for** $t = 1, ..., N_{req}$

   (a) For each $\mathbf{x}^* \in \mathcal{P}$ consider the average of log-likelihood for the next labeling request.

      i. Consider each possible label $\mathbf{z}^*$ for $\mathbf{x}^*$ and add the pair to the training set, $\mathcal{D}^* = \mathcal{D} \cup (\mathbf{x}^*, \mathbf{z}^*)$

      ii. Run EM given $\mathcal{D}^*$ to obtain model parameter $\hat{\mathbf{\Psi}}_{\mathcal{D}^*}$ for each possible label

      iii. Estimate the resulting log-likelihood using $\hat{\mathbf{\Psi}}_{\mathcal{D}^*}$ given $\mathcal{U} \equiv \mathcal{D}^* \cup \mathcal{P}$ using Eq. (6.4.4):

$$\tilde{\mathcal{L}}(\mathcal{U}|\hat{\mathbf{\Psi}}_{\mathcal{D}^*}) = \mathcal{L}(\mathcal{D}|\hat{\mathbf{\Psi}}_{\mathcal{D}^*}) + \mathcal{L}(\mathcal{P}|\hat{\mathbf{\Psi}}_{\mathcal{D}^*}).$$

      iv. Assign to $\mathbf{x}^*$ the average log-likelihood for each possible labeling $\mathbf{z}^*$ using Eq. (6.4.5):

$$\mathcal{E}_z[\tilde{\mathcal{L}}(\mathcal{U}|\hat{\mathbf{\Psi}}_{\mathcal{D}^*})] = \frac{1}{|\mathcal{C}|} \sum_{\mathbf{z}^* \in \mathcal{C}} \tilde{\mathcal{L}}(\mathcal{U}|\hat{\mathbf{\Psi}}_{\mathcal{D}^*}).$$

   (b) Select for labeling the example $\mathbf{x}^*$ with highest average log-likelihood on all other examples in $\mathcal{P}$.

   (c) Update training set and data pool: $\mathcal{D} \leftarrow \{\mathcal{D} \cup (\mathbf{x}_t^*, \mathbf{z}_t^*)\}$, $\mathcal{P} \leftarrow \{\mathcal{P} \backslash \mathbf{x}_t^*\}$

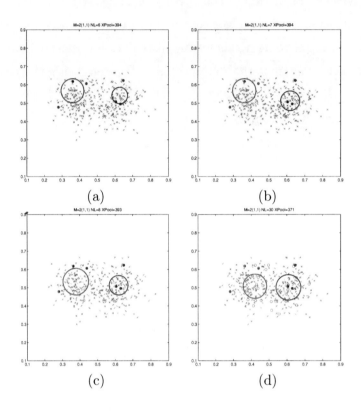

Figure 6.7: Illustration of query selections using the *Likelihood Increasing Sampling* (LIS) method. The simulation shows how the LIS method selects new examples when 2GAUSS data set is used for training. Here, we take simplest model that consists of two gaussian densities with spherical covariance parameters. In graph (a) the query process is begun by employing a weak model initialized using six labeled examples. In (b) a new example with the highest average likelihood is selected to be labeled and added to training set for next queries. The model after two new labeled examples added to the training set is showed in graph (c). The selected examples moved the center of gaussians to the position near centers of actual distribution. The graph of (d) shows the distribution of selected examples, centers and covariance of the gaussians after 30 queries.

We are aware that the whole process of this algorithm can be time-consuming. To make the algorithm more efficient and trackable, we may choose some of the following optimizations and approximations:

1. The expected log-likelihood can be estimated using only sub-sample of the pool of unlabeled data, especially when a large pool of unlabeled data is available.

2. When the EM algorithm needs large number of iteration to reach convergence condition, we can set a specific number of iterations in the computing of expected log-likelihood. For less complex models, fifty iteration of EM should be enough to get good estimates.

3. To avoid singularities in the EM, a regularizing of EM as introduced by Ormoneit and Tresp (Ormoneit & Tresp, 1998) can be employed by setting the regularizing factor ω_Σ to an arbitrary small constant.

6.4.2 Experimental Results

In this section the performance of the *Likelihood-Increasing Sampling* was evaluated in compare with passive learning and the *Expected Likelihood-based Sampling* method. For this purpose we used BANANA and HEART data set, benchmark collection selected and used by Rätsch et al. (Rätsch et al., 2001). The HEART data set contains 170 examples of 13-dimensions and was extracted from UCI repository (Blake & Merz, 1998). For all problems this collection includes fixed 100 folds, each consists of fixed 60%/40% training/test replication. In our experiments we used only up to 50 folds of the available folds due to the computation cost of LIS. For visualization purpose and a simple test, we created a two-dimension synthetical data set 2GAUSS with balance classes as also used in the previous section. All data sets are binary classification problems.

In our experiments we used gaussian mixture models with spherical covariance parameter and EM algorithm for estimating parameters of the models. In the figures below, we evaluate the generalization errors of test data sets. To cut computation cost, in this experiment during query process of the *Likelihood-Increasing Sampling*, the number of EM iteration was limited up to 50 iterations. For all methods we initialize EM using the K-means initialization given the current training data set. Centers of gaussians are initialized as the centroids of the Voronoi set found. The variance parameters are initialized as the variances corresponding to the data found in the Voronoi regions. For all experiments the algorithm was given 5 examples per mixture component as initial training set sampled at random from a given pool of unlabeled data. The number of mixture component for each class was selected using BIC criterion (Dasgupta & Raftery, 1998) with highest score.

Having a new selected example, the example is then added to current labeled training set for constructing classifier. The class-conditional densities was estimated using EM and it run until convergence is reached, i.e. the change in log-likelihood from one iteration to the next fell below 10^{-5}. The classification errors then are computed using test data sets. We compared three different active learning algorithms:

- Random - choosing the query example at random

- *Expected Likelihood-based Sampling* - the method introduced in the previous section - choosing the examples that minimize the expected likelihood as in equation (6.3.2).

- *Likelihood-Increasing Sampling* - the method introduced in this section - choosing the examples that maximize the average likelihood as in equation (6.4.5).

We first considered whether the *Likelihood-Increasing Sampling* method provides any benefit over random sampling. Furthermore *Expected*

Likelihood-based Sampling method was considered for the same data sets. The results of experiments are presented in the figures below.

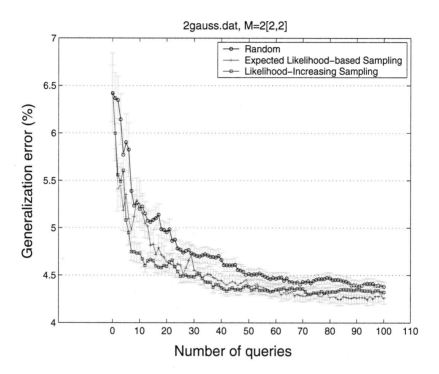

Figure 6.8: The result of experiment of the *Likelihood-Increasing Sampling* method using 2GAUSS data sets. **Horizontal-axis**: the number of queries. **Vertical-axis**: generalization error. In this experiment, the classifiers were built using $M = 2$ gaussian mixture components and initialized with five labeled examples for each class. The error bars denote the standard deviation about the mean of 50 trials.

The results of experiments obtained using 2GAUSS and BANANA data set are shown in Figure 6.8 and 6.9, respectively. In these experiments, we used only 25% of examples in the pool set as query candidate in the *Likelihood-Increasing Sampling*. We applied correct models (mixture of two-gaussians) in Figure 6.8 and mixture of 10 gaussians in Figure 6.9,

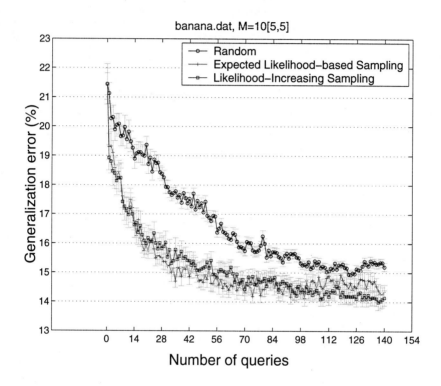

Figure 6.9: The result of experiment of the *Likelihood-Increasing Sampling* method using BANANA data sets. **Horizontal-axis**: the number of queries. **Vertical-axis**: generalization error. In this experiment, the classifiers were built using $M = 10[5, 5]$ gaussian mixture components and initialized with 25 labeled examples for each class. The error bars denote the standard deviation about the mean of 50 trials for both the Likelihood-Increasing Sampling and the passive method.

5 gaussians to model each class. Unfortunately, the correct model for BANANA data set are unknown, therefore here we estimated it using BIC criterion. The *Likelihood-Increasing Sampling* method performs substantially better than random selection method, as can be seen in both figures. The method shows better result in some points better than *Expected Likelihood-based Sampling* method e.g. in the Figure 6.8, especially when

the number of query is small.

In Figure 6.9 the *Likelihood-Increasing Sampling* method showed reducing classification error quickly in compare with random selection method. For example the algorithm reaches 15.1% error rate in 46 queries, while the passive method after choosing 123 queries, 2.67 times slower than the *Likelihood-Increasing Sampling* method. The similar performance also was shown by *Expected Likelihood-based Sampling* method. In this experiment *Likelihood-Increasing Sampling* does not show superiority over *Expected Likelihood-based Sampling* method. For this data set a better structure of the model should be considered.

Experiment using HEART data set was performed using mixture of two gaussians, one gaussian for each class. In this experiment, *Likelihood-Increasing Sampling* used only 100 of 170 available unlabeled data in the pool for querying. Again, first we compared the method with random selection method, then with *Expected Likelihood-based Sampling* method. From the Figure 6.10 we learn that the *Likelihood-Increasing Sampling* performs better than random selection method for all points. A fast increasing performance of the *Likelihood-Increasing Sampling* can be observed in the Figures 6.10, where the passive method needed minimal 100 queries to reach the same point in which the *Likelihood-Increasing Sampling* needs only 35 queries. The performance of the proposed algorithm could be increased by using all candidates for querying, so that more representative examples can be obtained. Moreover, the *Likelihood-Increasing Sampling* shows better than *Expected Likelihood-based Sampling* method.

6.4.3   Conclusion

In this section we proposed an active learning algorithm, the *Likelihood-Increasing Sampling*, by taking prior data distribution into account to

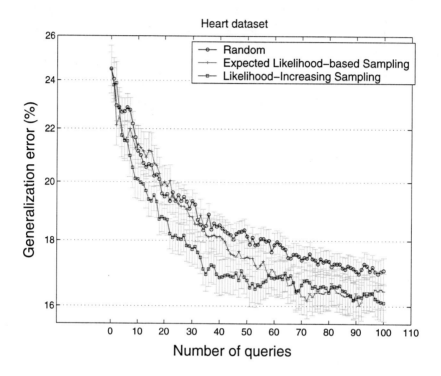

Figure 6.10: The result of experiment of the *Likelihood-Increasing Sampling* method using HEART data sets. **Horizontal-axis**: the number of queries. **Vertical-axis**: generalization error. In this experiment, the classifiers were built using mixture of two gaussians and given 10 labeled examples for initialization. The error bars denote the standard deviation about the mean of 30 trial for all, *Likelihood-Increasing Sampling*, random selection and *Expected Likelihood-based Sampling* method. In this experiment, *Likelihood-Increasing Sampling* used only 100 of 170 available unlabeled data in the pool for querying.

build optimal generative classifiers. Instead of choosing samples that close to the classification boundaries, the algorithm attempts to obtain representative examples whereby an optimal model can be constructed. The algorithm selects carefully a new example from a pool of unlabeled data that has largest contribution to the increasing of current likelihood. The pool of unlabeled data and collected labeled data are used to estimate future likelihood of the model and determine the impact of each potential labeling request on the expected likelihood. The method has been studied using benchmark data sets of binary classification problems. The results of experiments show efficiency (in context of query number) of the proposed algorithm in compare with random selection method.

This method has some advantage over previous method. Since the algorithm attempts to build optimal models by taking prior data distribution into account, the method will be more robust to the effect of noisy data. The method gives not only efficiency in reducing labeling cost, but also information about probabilistic measures of the data which could be useful for decision making tasks.

CHAPTER 7
Summary

Nowadays the machine learning plays an important role in many tasks of data analysis and pattern recognition. In this work two important tasks of machine learning, classification and density estimation, have been investigated. In classification, the task is to classify data points into one of a set of known classes, while in density estimation we attempt to approximate probability densities of the data. For both tasks we used mixture models and EM algorithm.

Mixture model is a standard method and used in statistics as a convenient semi-parametric way for modelling the probability density function. Using mixture model a probability density is represented as a linear combination of kernel densities. In this dissertation, the EM algorithm, a standard iterative algorithm for maximum-likelihood, was applied to find optimal parameters of the models.

The dissertation deals with learning problems of the mixture models, especially for kernels of gaussians. It consists of three different themes: (i) learning of the mixture models for density estimation; (ii) semi-supervised learning; and (iii) active learning for the gaussian mixture model-based classifiers.

In the first theme we investigated an initialization problem of EM for estimation of the gaussian mixture model parameters. This theme is motivated by the fact that EM is a local optimization algorithm and very sensitive to initialization. Usually to overcome this initialization dependence problem, the K-Means algorithm is used to determine initial positions for the gaussian mixture components. Since K-Means itself is a local method, the strong dependence on initialization persist. We therefore studied empirically this problem and investigated a possibility to remedy the problem by using the LBG-U algorithm (Fritzke, 1997).

LBG-U is generalization of the LBG (Linde *et al.*, 1980) algorithm for vector quantization problems. In contrast to the LBG, LBG-U shows only a weak dependence on initialization and generates in many cases codebooks with considerably lower quantization error. Some experiments have been performed to compare the performance of EM using three different techniques, random-, LBG-, and LBGU-initialization. The results of the performed experiments showed superiority of LBGU-EM in improving performance of EM compared with LBG and randomly initialized EM. Moreover, the LBGU-EM leads to lower variances of the resulting log-likelihood and thus to be better reliability of the results. The achieved means of negative log-likelihoods using LBGU-EM were lower than those of both LBG and randomly initialized EM. The experimental results showed that the proposed algorithm outperformed the other methods on the used data set. However, a better characterization of the data sets for which the LBGU-EM gives an improvement is still an open problem. Since the LBG-U minimizes a different objective function than density estimation, it may also be possible to create variance of LBG or

LBG-U which take this into account.

In the second theme we studied the *semi-supervised learning*, a combination of supervised and unsupervised learning, in which a classifier is trained not only using labeled data but also unlabeled data. This theme is known also as the labeled and unlabeled data problem. The motivation of this research is that the classification error of a classifier build by augmenting unlabeled data into a labeled training data set may be lower than the error of classification obtained when the classifier is build on the basis of the labeled data alone. In the other hand the obtaining of a large quantity of unlabeled data in many domains is very easy and cheap. This issue is of high interest and as an object of current researches in the machine learning due to their potential in reducing the labeled data, which are very expensive in many applications.

On this theme we focussed on a basic question, under which conditions the unlabeled data can help classification. Although some authors have reported their works on this theme, some questions remain unclear. Furthermore, our research was devoted to explore three different aspects. First, the effect of the unlabeled data on the model complexity. We considered a condition when the generative models have correct structure (their structure are same as underlying distributions that generated the data) and incorrect structure. Second, the effect of unlabeled data on overfitting condition. Special attention is given to observe, if unlabeled data can help to avoid overfitting. Finally, we presented a regularization method to adjust the strength of labeled/unlabeled data's contribution. For this case we proposed a novel method by weighting the log-likelihood using the *regularized* weighting factors. This method is useful when full complexity of data sets cannot be completely captured by mixture models. By adjusting the weighting parameter of unlabeled data an optimal classifier can be found. For all we conducted empirical studies by taking generalization error into account.

From the performed experiments some results were found. We observed that unlabeled data can *always* help classification when a generative model has a *correct* structure. For this case, a high performance can be achieved by augmenting a large number of unlabeled data. When a model has *incorrect* structure, however, the unlabeled data can *not always* help classification. We observed also that the unlabeled data can help classification although a classifier was constructed using an incorrect structure. Unlabeled data can, however, *degrade* performance when the generative models were constructed using a few mixture components and not enough to represent the underlying distribution. Another interesting result was observed that the unlabeled data can help to avoid *overfitting* condition. Our results also showed that the proposed regularization method can be used to control the strength of contribution of unlabeled data.

In the third theme, we studied a framework of machine learning so-called *active* learning. Generally the active learning aims to achieve high performance classifiers using as small number of labeled data as possible. In contrast to passive learning, in active learning a learner itself is responsible for acquiring the training examples, so that it can carefully select examples to be labeled. With this additional power it is expected that good performance of classifiers can be reached and the efforts of labeling can be reduced. Active learning methods are therefore very important in many practical setting, since procuring class labels can be costly and time-consuming.

In the literature some authors have been proposed the active learning algorithms using different classifiers. Most of them however attaint to select samples close to the current decision boundaries and give no attention to the the prior data distribution. In this dissertation we proposed novel active learning algorithms, the *Expected Likelihood-based Sampling* and *Likelihood-Increasing Sampling* for generative classifiers based on the gaussian mixture models. The algorithms take prior data distribution into account to construct classifiers. The algorithms work under pool-based learning, in which the learners have access to all possible queries.

The *Expected Likelihood-based Sampling* method attempts to find an optimal model with low computation cost. The method selects examples from the pool having the lowest expected likelihood. The expectation is evaluated using current model and an example candidate added to the training data set. Some experiments have been performed to compare the performance of the algorithm and random selection method. The results of the performed experiments showed superiority of the method in improving performance of classifiers based on gaussian mixture models compared with passive learning method. The results of experiments using four data sets indicate that the proposed method can reduce dramatically the number of labeled examples needed to achieve the same performance level of random selection method.

The *Likelihood-Increasing Sampling* method attempts to obtain representative examples whereby an optimal generative model can be constructed. The method selects carefully a new example from a pool of unlabeled data that has largest contribution to the increasing of current likelihood. We used the pool of unlabeled data and collected labeled data to estimate the likelihood of the estimated model and determine the impact of each potential labeling request on the expected likelihood. To reduce computation cost, we suggested some optimization techniques e.g. by using sub-sampling of the unlabeled data to generate a pool of candidates at each iteration. Since the method attempts to build optimal generative models, the method will be more robust to the effect of noisy data. The method gives not only efficiency in reducing labeling cost but also the constructed generative models can be used for decision making tasks that require information about probabilistic measures of the data.

The proposed active learning methods have not pay attention to singularities problem that may be occur during query selection process. For *Likelihood-Increasing Sampling* method that attempts to achieve optimal likelihood will choose wrong queries when singularities occurred in evaluating expected values of log-likelihood. In the future work, this problem will be investigated. Another direction for future research is the development of the proposed active learning methods for stream-based learning, in case the learner is given with a stream of unlabeled examples.

References

Akaike, H. 1974. A new look at the statistical model identification. *IEEE Transactions on Automatic Control*, **AC-19**(6), 716723.

Amari, Sun Ichi, Cichocki, Andrzej, & Yang, H.H. 1995. A new learning algorithm for blind signal separation. *In:* Touretzky, David S., Mozer, Michael C., & Hasselmo, Michael E. (eds), *Advances in Neural Information Processing Systems*, vol. 8. The MIT Press.

Angluin, Dana. 1988. Queries and concept learning. *Machine Learning*, **2**(4), 319–342.

Arabie, P., Hubert, L.J., & Soete, G. De. 1988. *Clustering and Classification*. River Edge , NJ: World Scrientific.

Argamon-Engelson, Shlomo, & Dagan, Ido. 1999. Committee-Based Sample Selection for Probabilistic Classifiers. *Journal of Artificial Intelligence Research*, **11**, 335–360.

Baluja, Shumeet. 1998. Probabilistic Modeling for Face Orientation Discrimination: Learning from Labeled and Unlabeled Data. *Neural Information Procesing systems (NIPS '98)*.

Banfield, J. D., & Raftery, A. E. 1993. Model-based Gaussian and non-Gaussian clustering. *Biometrics*, **49**, 803–821.

Barabino, N., Pallavicini, M., Petrolini, A., Pontil, M., & Verri, A. 1999. Support vector machines vs multi-layer perceptrons in particle identification. *Pages 257–262 of:* Verleysen, M. (ed), *Proceedings ESANN*. D Facto.

Bishop, C. 1995. *Neural Networks for Pattern Recognition.* New York: Oxford University Press.

Blake, C.L., & Merz, C.J. 1998. *UCI Repository of machine learning databases.* [http://www.ics.uci.edu/~mlearn/MLRepository.html]. University of California, Irvine, Dept. of Information and Computer Sciences.

Brown, M. P. S., Grundy, W. N., Lin, D., Cristianini, N., Sugnet, C., Purey, T. S., Ares, M., & Haussler, D. 2000. Knowledge-based analysis of microarray gene expression data using support vector machines. *Pages 262–267 of: Proceedings of the National Academy of Sciences 97(2).*

Bruce, Rebecca. 2001. A Bayesian Approach to Semi-Supervised Learning. *Pages 57–64 of: Proceedings of the Sixth Natural Language Processing Pacific Rim Symposium, November 27-30, 2001, Hitotsubashi Memorial Hall, National Center of Sciences, Tokyo, Japan.*

Campbell, Colin, Cristianini, Nello, & Smola, Alex. 2000. Query Learning with Large Margin Classifiers. *Pages 111–118 of: Proceedings 17th International Conference on Machine Learning (ICML).* Morgan Kaufmann, CA.

Castelli, Vittorio, & Cover, Thomas M. 1995. On the exponential value of labeled samples. *Pattern Recognition Letters*, **16**, 105–111.

Castelli, Vittorio, & Cover, Thomas M. 1996. The Relative Value of Labeled and Unlabeled Samples in Pattern Recognition with an Unknown Mixing Parameter. *IEEE Trans. Information Theory*, **42**(Nov), 2102 – 2117.

Celeux, G., & Govaert, G. 1995. Gaussian parsimonious clustering model. *Pattern Recognition*, **28**, 781–793.

Chapelle, Oliver, Schölkopf, B., & Weston, J. 2002. *Semi-supervised learning through principle directions estimation.* Tech. rept. Max Plank Institute, Germany.

Cohen, Ira, Sebe, N., Cozman, Fabio G., Cirelo, M. C., & Huang, T. S. 2003. Learning Bayesian network classifiers for facial expression recognition using both labeled and unlabeled data. *In: IEEE Computer Society Conference on Pattern Recognition.*

Cohn, David A. 1994. Neural network exploration using optimal experiment design. *Page 679686 of:* Cowan, J., Tesauro, G., & Alspector, J. (eds), *Advances in neural information processing systems,* vol. 6. San Mateo, CA: Morgan Kaufmann.

Cohn, David A. 1997. Minimizing statistical bias with queries. *Page 417423 of:* Mozer, M. C., Jordan, M., & Petsche, T. (eds), *Advances in neural information processing systems 9.* Cambridge, MA: MIT Press.

Cohn, David A., Atlas, Les, & Ladner, Richard E. 1994. Improving Generalization with Active Learning. *Machine Learning,* **15**(2), 201–221.

Cohn, David A., Ghahramani, Z., & Jordan, M. I. 1995. Active learning with statistical models. *Pages 705–712 of:* Tesauro, G., Touretzky, D., & Leen, T. (eds), *Advances in Neural Information Processing Systems,* vol. 7. MIT Press.

Cozman, Fabio G., & Cohen, Ira. 2001. *Unlabeld Data Can Degrade Classification Performance of Generative Classifiers.* Tech. rept. HP Laboratories.

Cozman, Fabio Gagliardi, Cohen, Ira, & Cirelo, Marcelo Cesar. 2003. Semi-Supervised Learning of Mixture Models. *In: Proceedings of the Twentieth International Conference on Machine Learning (ICML-2003).*

Dasgupta, A., & Raftery, A. E. 1998. Detecting feature in spatial processes with cluster via model-based clustering. *American Statistical Association,* **93**, 294–302.

Dasgupta, Sonjay. 1999. Learning Mixtures of Gaussians. *In: IEEE Symposium on Foundations Computer Science (FOCS) 1999.*

Dempster, A. P., Laird, N. M., & Rubin, D. B. 1977. Maximum likelihood from incomplete data via the EM algorithm. *Journal of the Roy. Stat. Soc., Ser.B*, **39**, 1–38.

Devijver, P. A., & Kittler, J. V. 1982. *Pattern Recognition. Statistical Approach.* N.J: Prentice Hall, Englewood Cliffs.

Devroye, L., Gy"orfi, L., & Lugosi, G. 1996. *Probabilistic Theory of Pattern Recognition.* New York: Springer.

Dietterich, T.G. 2003. Machine Learning.

Domingos, P. 2000. Bayesian averaging of classifiers and the overfitting problem. *Page 223230 of: Proceedings of the International Conference on Machine Learning (ICML).*

Duda, R.O., Hart, P.E., & Stork, D.G. 2000. *Pattern Classification.* second edn. New York: John Wiley & Sons.

Dundar, M. Murat, & Landgrebe, David. 2002. A Model Based Mixture Supervised Classification Approach in Hyperspectral Data Analysis. *IEEE Transactions on Geoscience and Remote Sensing*, **40**(11), 269–2699.

Efron, B., & Tibshirani, B. 1993. *An introduction to bootstrap.* New York: Chapman and Hall.

Fayyad, U. M., Piatetsky-Shapiro, G., Smyth, P., & Uthurusamy, R. 1995. *Advance in Knowledge Discovery and Data Mining.* CA: Press.

Fedorov, V. V. 1972. *Theory of optimal experiments.* New York: Academic Press.

Flury, B.W., Schmid, M.J., & Narayanan, A. 1993. Error rates in quadratic discrimination with constraints on the covariance matrices. *Journal of Classification*, **11**, 101–120.

Fraley, Chris, & Raftery, Adrian E. 1998. How Many Clusters? Which Clustering Method? Answers Via Model-Based Cluster Analysis. *The Computer Journal*, **41**(8), 578–588.

Freund, Yoav, Seung, H. Sebastian, Shamir, Eli, & Tishby, Naftali. 1997. Selective Sampling Using the Query by Committee Algorithm. *Machine Learning*, **28**(2-3), 133–168.

Fritzke, Bernd. 1997. The LBG-U Method for Vector Quantization - an Improvement over LBG Inspired from Neural Network. *Neural Processing Letters*, **5, No. 1**, 35–45.

Fritzke, Bernd. 1998. *Vektorbasierte Neuronale Netze*. Aachen: Shaker.

Fukumizu, K. 1996. Active learning in multilayer perceptrons. *Page 295301 of:* Touretzky, D., Mozer, M., & Hasselmo, M. (eds), *Advances in neural information processing systems*, vol. 8. Cambridge: MIT Press.

Fukunaga, K. 1990. *Introduction to Statistical Pattern Recognition*. 2nd edn. Boston: Academic Press.

Ganesalingam, S., & McLachlan, G. 1978. The efficiency of a linear discriminant function based on unclassified initial samples. *Biometrika*, **65**, 658–662.

Ganesalingam, S., & McLachlan, G. 1979. Small sample results for a linear discriminant function estimated from a mixture of normal populations. *Journal of Statistical Computation and Simulation*, **9**, 151–158.

Geman, S., Bienenstock, E., & Doursat, R. 1992. Neural networks and the bias/variance dilemma. *Neural Computation*, 4(1), 158.

Gersho, A., & Gray, R. M. 1992. *Vector Quantization and Signal Compression*. Norwell: Kluwer.

Ghahramani, Z., & Jordan, M.I. 1994. Function approximation via density estimation using the EM approach. *Pages 120–127 of:* Cowan, J.D., Tesauro, G., & Alspector, J. (eds), *Advance in Neural Information Processing System 6*. San Mateo, CA: Morgan Kaufmann.

Hasenjäger, Martina. 2000. *Active Data Selection for Supervised and Unsupervised Learning*. Ph.D. thesis, Universität Bielefeld.

Hasenjäger, Martina, & Ritter, Helge. 1998. Active Learning with Local Models. *Neural Processing Letters*, **7**, 107–117.

Hasenjäger, Martina, Ritter, Helge, & Obermayer, Klaus. 1999. Active learning in self-organizing maps. *Pages 57–70 of:* Oja, E., & Kaski, S. (eds), *Kohonan Maps.* Amsterdam: Elsevier.

Iswanto, Bambang Heru, & Fritzke, Bernd. 2002. LBGU-EM Algorithm for Mixture Density Estimation. *Pages 252–261 of:* Schader, M., Gaul, W., & Vichi, M. (eds), *Between Data Science and Applied Data Analysis: The 26th Annual Conference of the German Classification Society.* Springer Verlag, Heidelberg.

Jain, A. K., & Dubes, R. C. 1988. *Algorthms for Clustering Data.* NJ: Prentice-Hall Englewood Cliffs.

Jain, A. K., & Pankanti, S. 2001. Automatic Fingerprint Identification Systems. *Pages 275–326 of:* Gaensslen, R.E., & Lee, H. (eds), *Advances in Fingerprint Sciences.* CRC Press.

Jain, A. K., Ross, A., & Prabhakar, S. 2004. An Introduction to Biometric Recognition. *IEEE Trans. on Circuits and Systems for Video Technology Special Issue on Image- and Video-Based Biometrics,* **14**(1), 4–20.

Jain, A.K., Murty, M.N., & Flynn, P.J. 1999. Data clustering: a review. *ACM Computing Surveys,* **31**(3), 264–323.

Joachims, T. 1998. Text categorization with support vector machines: Learning with many relevant features. *Pages 137–142 of: Proceedings of the European Conference on Machine Learning.* Berlin: Springer.

Jutten, C., & Heraut, J. 1991. Blind separation of sources 1: An adaptive algorithm based on neuromimetic architecture. *Signal Processing,* **24**(1), 1–10.

Keysers, D., Dahmen, J., Ney, H., Wein, B., & Lehmann, T. 2003. Statistical Framework for Model-based Image Retrieval in Medical Applications. *Pages 59–68 of: Journal of Electronic Imaging (Special Section on Model-based Medical Image Processing and Analysis),* vol. 12 No. 1.

Kohonen, Teuvo. 2001. *Self-Organizing Maps.* third edn. Heidelberg: Springer Verlag.

LeCun, Y., Buttou, L.D., Brunot, A., Cortes, C., Denker, J.S., Drucker, H., Guyon, I., Muller, U.A., Sackinger, E., Simard, P., & Vapnik, V. 1995. Comparison of learning algorithms for handwritten digit recognition. *Pages 53–60 of: International Conference on Arificial Neural Networks.*

Lewis, David D., & Catlett, Jason. 1994. Heterogeneous uncertainty sampling for supervised learning. *Pages 148–156 of:* Cohen, William W., & Hirsh, Haym (eds), *Proceedings of ICML-94, 11th International Conference on Machine Learning.* New Brunswick, US: Morgan Kaufmann Publishers, San Francisco, US.

Lewis, David D., & Gale, William A. 1994. A sequential algorithm for training text classifiers. *Pages 3–12 of:* Croft, W. Bruce, & van Rijsbergen, Cornelis J. (eds), *Proceedings of SIGIR-94, 17th ACM International Conference on Research and Development in Information Retrieval.* Dublin, IE: Springer Verlag, Heidelberg, DE.

Linde, Y., Bujo, A., & Gray, R. M. 1980. An algorithm for vector quantizer design. *IEEE Transaction on Communication,* **COM-28**, 84–95.

Little, R.J.A., & Rubin, D.B. 1987. *Statistical Analysis with Missing Data.* New York: Wiley.

MacKay, D.J.C. 1992. Information-based objective functions for active data selection. *Neural Computation,* **4**(4), 590604.

Maram, Yoran, El-Yaniv, Ran, & Luz, Kobi. 2004. Online Choice of Active Learning Algorithms. *Machine Learning Research,* **5**, 255–291.

McCallum, Andrew, & Nigam, Kamal. 1998. Employing EM and Pool-Based Active Learning for Text Classification. *Pages 359–367 of: Machine Learning: Proceedings of the Fifteenth International Conference (ICML '98).*

McLachlan, G. J., & Basford, K. E. 1988. *Mixture Models: Inference and Applications to Clustering.* New York: Marcel Dekker.

McLachlan, G. J., & Peel, D. 2000. *Finite Mixture Models.* Canada: John Wiley & Sons.

McLachlan, G.J., & Gordon, R.D. 1989. Mixture models for partially unclassified data: a case study of renal venous renin levels in essential hypertention. *Statistics in Medicine*, 1291–1300.

Meila, M., & Heckerman, D. 1998. *An Experimental Comparison of Several Clustering and Initialization Methods*. Tech. rept. MSR-TR-98-06. Microsoft Research.

Michie, D., Spiegelhalter, D.J., & (eds), C.C. Taylor. 1994. *Machine Learning, Neural and Statistical Classification*. New York: Ellis Horwood.

Miller, David J., & Browning, John. 2003. A Mixture Model and EM-Based Algorithm for Class Discovery, Robust Classification, and Outlier Rejection in Mixed Labeled/Unlabeled Sets. *IEEE Transaction on Pattern Analysis and Machine Intelligence*, **25**(11), 1468–1483.

Miller, David J., & Uyar, Hasan. 1996. A Mixture of Experts Classifier with Learning Based on Both Labelled and Unlabelled Data. *Advances in Neural Information Processing (NIPS-9)*, 571–577.

Mitchel, Tom. 1982. Generalization as search. *Artificial Intelligence*, **18**, 203–226.

Mitchell, Tom. 1997. *Machine Learning*. USA: McGraw-Hill.

Mitra, P., Murthy, C., & Pal, S. 2002. Density Based Multiscale Data Condensation. *IEEE Transactions on Pattern Analysis and Machine Intelligence*, **24**(6).

Moore, Andrew, Schneider, Jeff, Boyan, Justin, & Lee, Mary Soon. 1998. Q2: Memory-based active learning for optimizing noisy continuous functions. *Pages 386–394 of:* Shavlik, J. (ed), *Proceedings of the Fifteenth International Conference of Machine Learning*. 340 Pine Street, 6th Fl., San Francisco, CA 94104: Morgan Kaufmann.

Nabney, I.T. 2002. *Netlab: Algorithms for Pattern Recognition*. UK: Springer.

Nguyen, Hieu T., & Smeulders, Arnold. 2004. Active Learning Using Pre-clustering. *In: Proceedings 21th International Conference on Machine Learning (ICML)*.

Nigam, Kamal. 2001. *Using unlabeled data to improve text classi- fication.* Tech. rept. School of Computer Science, Carnegie Mellon University, Pennsylvania.

Nigam, Kamal, McCallum, Andrew, Thrun, Sebastian, & Mitchell, Tom. 2000. Text Classification from Labeled and Unlabeled Documents using EM. 103–134.

O'Neill, T.J. 1978. Normal discrimination with unclassified observations. *Journal of the American Statistical Association,* **73**, 821–826.

Ormoneit, D., & Tresp, V. 1998. Averaging, maximum penalized likelihood and Bayesian estimation for improving Gaussian mixture probability density estimates. *IEEE Transactions on Neural Networks,* **9(4)**, 639–650.

Ormoneit, Dirk, & Tresp, Volker. 1996. Improved Gaussian Mixture Density Estimates Using Bayesian Penalty Terms and Network Averaging. *Pages 542–548 of:* Touretzky, David S., Mozer, Michael C., & Hasselmo, Michael E. (eds), *Advances in Neural Information Processing Systems,* vol. 8. The MIT Press.

Portilla, J., Strela, V., Wainwright, M.J., & Simoncelli, E.P. 2003. Image denoising using scale mixture of Gaussians in the wavelet domain. *IEEE Transaction on Image Processing,* **12**(11), 1338–1351.

Povinelli, Richard J., Johnson, Michael T., & Lindgren, Andrew C. 2004. Time Series Classification Using Gaussian Mixture Models of Reconstructed Phase Spaces. *IEEE Transaction on Knowledge and Data Engineering,* **16**(6), 779–783.

Raab, G.M., & Elton, R.A:. 1993. Bayesian analysis of binary data from an audit of cervical smears. *Statistics Medicine,* **12**, 2179–2189.

Ratsaby, J., & Venkatesh, S.S. 1995. Learning from a mixture of labeled and unlabeled examples with parametric side information. 412–417.

Rätsch, G. http://horn.first.gmd.de/~ raetsch/data/benschmarks.htm.

Rätsch, G., Onoda, T., & Müller, K.R. 2001. Soft margin for Adaboost. *Machine Learning,* **42**, 287–320.

Redner, R. A., & Walker, H. F. 1984. Mixture densities, maximum-likelihood, and the EM algorithm. *SIAM Review*, **26**, 195–239.

Ripley, Brian D. 1996. *Pattern Recognition and Neural Networks*. Cambridge, UK: Cambridge University Press.

Roy, Nicholas, & McCallum, Andrew. 2001. Toward Optimal Active Learning through Sampling Estimation of Error Reduction. *Pages 441–448 of: Proc. 18th International Conf. on Machine Learning*. Morgan Kaufmann, San Francisco, CA.

Saar-Tsechansky, Maytal, & Provost, Foster. 2004. Active Sampling for Class Probability Estimation and Ranking. *Machine Learning*, **54**(2), 153–178.

Schohn, Greg, & Cohn, David. 2000. Less is More: Active Learning with Support Vector Machines. *Pages 839–846 of: Proc. 17th International Conf. on Machine Learning*. Morgan Kaufmann, San Francisco, CA.

Scott, D.W. 1992. *Multivariate Density Estimation*. New York: Wiley.

Seeger, Matthias. 2001. *Learning with Labeled and Unlabeled Data*. Tech. rept. Edinburgh University, UK.

Seeger, Matthias, & Williams, C. 2003. Fast forward selection to speed up sparse Gaussian process regression. *In: In Workshop on AI and Statistics 9*.

Seo, Sambu, & Obermayer, Klaus. 2003. Soft learning vector quantization. *Neural Compututaion*, **15**, 1589–1604.

Seung, H. S., Opper, Manfred, & Sompolinsky, Haim. 1992. Query by Committee. *Pages 287–294 of: Computational Learning Theory*.

Shahshahani, B., & Landgrebe, D. 1994. The effect of unlabeled samples in reducing the small sample size problem and mitigating the Hughes phenomenon. *IEEE Trans. Geoscience and Remote Sensing*, **32 (5)**, 10871095.

Simula, O., Ahola, J., Alhoniemi, E., Himberg, J., & Vesanto, J. 1999. Self-Organizing map in analysis of large-scale industrial systems.

Pages 375–387 of: E.Oja, & Kaski, S. (eds), *Kohonen Maps.* Elsevier.

Sixtus, A., Molau, S., Kanthak, S., Schlüter, R., & Ney, Hermann. 2000. Recent Improvements of the RWTH Large Vocabulary Speech Recognition System on Spontaneous Speech. *Pages 1671–1674 of: IEEE International Conference on Acoustics, Speech and Signal Processing.*

Sollich, P. 1992. Query construction, entropy and generalization in neural network models. *Physical Review E*, **49**, 46374651.

Sugiyama, Masashi, & Ogawa, Hidemitsu. 2000. Incremental Active Learning for Optimal Generalization. *Neural Computation*, **12**, 2909–2940.

Titterington, D. M., Smith, A. F. M., & Makov, U. E. 1985. *Statistical Analysis of Mixture Distributions.* Chichester: Wiley.

Tong, S., & Chang, Edward. 2001. Support vector machine active learning for image retrieval. *ACM Multimedia.*

Tong, S., & Koller, D. 2001a. Active learning for parameter estimation in Bayesian networks. *Pages 647–653 of: Advances in Neural Information Processing Systems*, vol. 13.

Tong, S., & Koller, D. 2001b. Support vector machine active learning with applications to text classification. *Machine Learning Research*, **2**, 45–66.

Tong, Simon. 2001. *Active Learning: Theory and Applications.* Ph.D. thesis, Stanford University.

Usama Fayyad, Cory Reina, & Bradley, Paul. 1998. Initialization of Iterative Refinement Clustering Algorithms. *In: The Fourth International Conference on Knowledge Discovery and Data Mining.*

Valiant, L. G. 1984. A theory learnable. *Communications of the ACM*, **27**(11), 1134–1142.

Vapnik, Vladimir. 1998. *Statistical Learning Theory.* New York: John Willey and Sohn.

Vapnik, Vladimir. 2000. *The Nature of Statistical Learning Theory*. second edn. Heidelberg: Springer Verlag.

Vijayakumar, S., & Ogawa, H. 1999a. Improving generalization ability through active learning. *IEICE Transactions on Information and Systems*, **E82-D(2)**, 480487.

Vijayakumar, S., & Ogawa, H. 1999b. Improving generalization ability through active learning. *IEICE Transactions on Information and Systems*, **E82D**(2), 480–487.

Wolberg, W. H., Street, W. N., & Mangasarian, O. L. 1994. Machine Learning Techniques to Diagnose Breast Cancer from Image-Processed Nuclear Features of Fine Needle Aspirates. *Cancer Letters*, **77**, 163–171.

Xu, Lei. 1997. Comparative Analysis on Convergence Rate of The EM Algorithm and Its Two Modifications for Gaussian Mixtures. *Neural Processing Letters*, **6**, 69–76.

Xu, Lei, & Jordan, Michael I. 1996. On convergence properties of the EM algorithm for Gaussian mixtures. *Neural Computation*, 129–151.

Zhang, Tong, & Oles, Frank. 2000. A probability analysis on the value of unlabeled data for classification problems. *Pages 1191–1198 of: International Join Conference on Machine Learning*.